WOF
W

ANGELS
AND
NATURE
SPIRITS

All Angels and Tree, Flower,
Animal & Mineral Nature Spirits

Dear Vicki and David
All my fondest love, thanks,
By and Angel
blessings

Lorna Todd *Lorna*

19.5.99.

Published by:

Kima Global Publishers,
P.O.Box 374,
Rondebosch
7701
Cape Town
South Africa

First Edition December 1998

© Lorna Todd 1998

Website: **http://www.globalvisions.org/cl/kima.**
e-mail: **kima@gem.co.za**

ISBN 0-9584065-9-6

Contents

SECTION THREE:

Nature Spirits of the Animal Kingdom
Base Centre

Sacral Centre

Heart Centre

Throat Centre

Brow Centre

Crown Centre

SECTION FOUR

Nature Spirits of the Mineral Kingdom

This book is dedicated to my husband Peter, with love and grateful thanks for all his help, patience and encouragement, and also to all my Angel friends, both human and etheric.

Introduction

This book has been written with great love and is dedicated to the Angelic and Nature kingdoms. As a child I was able to see the light of angels and Nature Spirits, but I must tell my readers that there is nothing special about me, or my abilities. With practice, anyone of you will be able to sense, see and commune with these glorious beings of light. Look on it as a journey, an adventure, each day bringing you closer to their essence and their unconditional love. The only key that you need is LOVE from the heart and a strong belief in their existence.

To commence your journey, have an ANGEL DAY, or several days. As soon as you awaken in the morning, bring Angels into your thoughts and your inner vision. All through the day notice how many instances arise when you see the written word 'Angels', or someone mentions Angels, or you see a beautiful ornament depicting their form. By the end of the day you will be amazed at how many incidents have been brought to your attention.

Use the next few weeks to sit quietly and let your imagination perceive their presence. Imagination is one of the greatest gifts that God has bestowed upon us. What you see with your imagination, or inner vision, soon becomes reality and Angels will enhance all parts of your everyday experiences. There is no need for deep meditation – just close your eyes, relax, and call the Angels into your awareness: for instance, Angels of Love, Angels of Peace, Angels of Healing, Angels of Protection or Angels of Forgiveness. If you have had a bad day and you are experiencing anger, then call to the Angel of Peace and let the essence of this Angel change your negative to positive, filling you with tranquility. Welcome Angels with love

1

from your heart and you will sense a shift in the atmosphere around you. You may become aware of a gentle touch on the crown of your head. Let their energy flow into your heart and body, and with your inner eyes you may behold the vision of a form. I always see Angels flowing with light, but a friend of mine always glimpses them with magnificent feathered wings. I am sure that Angels show themselves as we wish to perceive them. I have added little meditations throughout this book, which will help you to become more familiar with their glory.

Most people view Archangels as too far removed from humanity to come into their consciousness. This is not so. Humanity is at last opening up to the love and light of their Creator, and the Archangels are here to help us to reflect this light within ourselves, allowing us to claim our true birthright. I would urge all my Readers to get to know the names of the Archangels. The Bible mentions quite a few, including Gabriel, Michael, Raphael, Uriel, Ariel etc. Sit in a favourite chair where there is peace, or go into the garden or a field. Call the name of an Archangel and let the sound resonate from your heart, and you may again feel a gentle touch on your head. If you have summoned Raphael the Archangel of Healing, for instance, your body will soon become filled with the healing energy of that great being. Gabriel will replenish you with unconditional love, and Michael with strength and protection.

The clouds are wonderful mediums for beholding Angel forms. Last year, on a September evening, I was with a group of people performing a fire ritual. The sun was going down over the horizon, and twilight was almost upon us. Suddenly several of us looked up into the sky and saw that the clouds had formed into the figures of four illustrious Angels. One of then was Michael, holding aloft his flaming sword of light. Behind him flowed three more magnificent beings of light, all part of his glorious company of heavenly hosts. I said "Something awesome is about to happen!!", and a few hours later, at 2 a.m. the following morning, Princess Diana took her last breath and passed into the light. The Archangels and Angels were there to welcome her. The heavenly choir were singing songs of joy and hope. With her passing, Diana opening many heart centres that would have remained closed and barren, but for her sacrifice.

I recently read a beautiful story of a Grandmother whose Grandchild had recently died. For many months this dear lady and her daughter were unable to come to terms with their grief. However, one afternoon the Grandmother was sitting in her garden, when she too looked up into the sky. The clouds performed a miracle of love and compassion. She saw the figure of an Angel cradling in her arms the form of a small child. The Grandmother knew, without doubt, that this was her Grandchild, who was safe and secure with the Angels. Her grieving became less and she was able to take up her life once more.

As you move through the pages of this book, work with the Angels that I have mentioned and then invoke a few of your own. Listen with your mind and you too will hear their words, for they are truly Messengers of God and Builders of Form on every level.

I have just become conscious of a great Archangel, known as the Angel of the Presence. This is the Angel of our Higher Selves, the Angel of our Spirits. This being of light resides close to the heart of God, and is very joyous to now be able to draw near to humanity. As we continue to work to expand our hearts and our minds, the Angel of the Presence will bring to us many words of wisdom. This truth will be very familiar, as it is knowledge that we have learned from previous lives spent on earth and in other Galaxies and Solar Systems.

All over the Universe are Angelic forces – of such magnitude, that we cannot even begin to perceive their glory. Many of them are drawing close to Earth, to witness what is happening to this beautiful, but small, planet on the outer reaches of Space. All of creation on Mother Earth is rising into light – we are going home – back to the heart of our Creator.

It is common knowledge that when the Astronauts first went to the Moon, they looked out of their capsule and saw gigantic Angels escorting them on their mission. When they returned to Earth, every one of them had altered in some way. This is what is occurring to Humanity and this planet – we are transforming and changing into CHILDREN OF GOD – we are coming into our own light and power.

I hope you will enjoy this small book and that each one of you will feel the love of the Angels flowing from the pages. Hold your hand over the cover of this book, and you will experience the energy of the Angels love and healing power surging into your palm.

May the Joy of their blessings
And the light of their countenance
Illumine your Path,
As you journey back to your true home
WITHIN THE HEART OF GOD.

Section One

ANGELS OF LIGHT

Some insist angels don't exist
But I have seen them fly
High up in the deep blue sky,
Trailing wings like mist, moon kissed.
Their raiments floating, swaying
Softly as a lacy veil, changing,
Blown by the breeze where'ere it lists.

Two there were with outstretched wings,
Bringing a message of heavenly things.
(faintly I hear a choir that sings.)
With Godly grace
All space rings,
And joy and peace abound
With awe I saw...
And stood spellbound.

Hope Denoon

ANGELS

Recently, with great joy, I flew into Perth to start a nine week tour of Australia and New Zealand. Angels greeted me as soon as I set foot on that fair land. I was travelling to Busseldon to take an Angel Workshop and wanted to link with Dolphins on the way. There were four of us in a camper van and, quite spontaneously, it was suggested that we stop at the small town called Bunbury. We stood on a slight hill and looked into the sea. We did not see dolphins, but someone noticed that there was writing in the glorious white sand. There were two words, written in joined up letters, and to our amazement those two words read "CHEERS LORNA". What a wonderful welcome that was from the Angels of Light. Once you bring angels into your life, life is never quite the same again.

There was a time, not so long ago, when you would have been considered mad, or at the very least eccentric, if you spoke of the existence of angels and the fairy kingdom. Fortunately, they are now the theme of television programmes and articles in the daily newspapers. There are more and more people able to 'tell' of their experiences without sensure or ridicule. Stories are told about angel intervention, and guardian angels that have averted accidents and negative occurrences.

A few years ago a man asked if he could talk to me about angels. He was very nervous, and when I questioned him it transpired that as a young boy the vision of an angel had appeared at the foot of his bed. He had been reading a book and assured me that he had not been asleep. He described the angel as a bright light with very little form.

From the centre of this vision, bands of golden energy had filled the whole of his bedroom.

After this experience, however, he had been unable to discuss it with anybody. Instead of appreciating what a divine presence he had encountered, it played upon his mind until he thought that he was going insane. When he came to see me he was in his early forties, and the event was still as fresh in his mind as the day he saw his angel. All through those years he had felt that he was 'not right in the head'. I talked to him for several hours and assured him that he was quite 'normal'. I told him of my own experiences and explained to him the glory of the angelic realms. How sad that such a wonderful event, instead of awakening him to spiritual truth, had been the source of unending worry and sadness. Angels come to us with so much love, and are waiting patiently to be of service. I believe that we are standing on the brink of a new beginning, when mankind will once again tune in to these beings of light in order to aid his spiritual journey.

Angels are not a new concept, they have been with us since we left the heart of God as small sparks of light to begin our long journey into physical manifestation. Before we could live on Mother Earth, we had to start the construction of our other bodies, spiritual, mental, astral and etheric. A vast army of angelic hosts drew near to our earth, many having traveled from other universes. They came because of their love for those tiny sparks of light who would eventually become individuals with the power of free will. Very few inhabitants of planets have been granted this privilege, which has been bestowed upon us by the God of our universe in order to accomplish one small part of his divine plan. Seraphim and Cherubim, Lords of the Flame, Lords of Wisdom, Form and Mind, archangels and angels were all drawn to Planet Earth over vast periods of time, until man was able to stand on his own two feet and become a feeling, thinking individual – a God in the making. We can have no conception of the glory of these visitors, but I feel sure that as we journey back to the heart of God these companions will be with us to witness our triumph.

When you attract Angels into your consciousness, life becomes filled with joy and happiness. From early childhood I have tuned into the essence of Angels and Nature Spirits and within the pages of this book, I will bring to my readers the magic of their words.

Whenever I see Angels, either with my inner vision or with my physical eyes, they show themselves to me as pure white or golden light. There is an outline of form with a heart centre that is pouring out unconditional love and healing rays into our world. Their eyes are always filled with sympathy and compassion. Angels cannot understand why we have so much difficulty with the word 'love'. For them it is so simple, but for mankind so very complicated.

Angels will help us with every experience that we encounter from day to day. We only have to ask and they will come to our assistance. There are Angels of money, Angels of relationships, Angels who will work with computers and Angels who will help us with our children. I would urge you to open the door of your home to these divine messengers and bring harmony into your everyday living. Make a small altar somewhere in your home to honour these beings of light. Place a picture and some flowers in this space and the angels will praise and favour you in return. When you enter a friend's house, greet the Angel of that hearth and bless all that reside within the walls.

I would encourage all my readers to welcome Angels into their meditations and prayers. In this way you will discover the great love which awaits you from the angelic stream. Let tenderness and kindness rule your thinking, let gentleness and peace be your goal, so that the vibrations of the Angels may shed light before you, as you walk the paths of human experience.

THE ARCHANGELS

On higher levels of awareness dwell beings of pure light, who are called ARCHANGELS. These perfect expressions of God's will, power and love have a higher rank than angels, and serve larger areas of human life. Many of these wondrous light bearers, from other parts of the Universe, are drawing close to our world. They are coming to help and experience the great leap in consciousness that is about to happen to humanity as we enter the golden age of ascension and transformation.

Although Archangels are neither male nor female, they each have a feminine counterpart. For example:

MICHAEL AND FAITH – Leaders of the heavenly host of Angels and Archangels.

JOPHIEL AND CHRISTINE – Who bring love through wisdom to humanity.

GABRIEL AND HOPE – Who represent the trumpet or voice of God.

RAPHAEL AND MOTHER MARY – Who bring divine healing to humanity.

URIEL AND AURORA – Who represent the fire of God.

ZADKIEL AND AMETHYST – Who represent the mystery and ritual of God.

There is one particular Archangel who is serving humanity at this present time, and is known as **METATRON – King of Angels and the tallest Angel in Heaven.** He is drawing close to mankind to help all people of the world to ascend into the light of the golden age.

When Metatron first appeared in my meditations, he came as a vast column of light. So bright that I dared not look fully upon his countenance. He gave me the following message for humanity:

"Be at peace. I bring you love and compassion from the heart of God. I am a part of that great energy, just as all of you are a part of the Creator. We are all one, there is no separation. You are unified with every atom of this Universe. Every star, solar system and tiny grain of sand is your brother and your sister. Within your hearts is all knowledge, all wisdom and all truth.

"I bring to your Planet the beautiful energies and vibrations for the Golden Age, which has now commenced. Accept your birthrights and awaken to the vision of your own divinity. Many souls wished to enter Earth at this time, and you were chosen. So harken to my words, and join the band of light bearers who are holding aloft their flaming torches to burn away darkness, so that your whole Planet will become an orb of brilliant light.

"You only have to call my name and I will be with you. Let my energies dissolve all disharmony, all fear, all anger. I have a silver cloak of protection, which I will place around your shoulder. Put your hand in mine, and we will walk the path of unconditional love together.

"Bring me into your meditations and let my name be on your lips before you sleep. In this way I can take you up into the spiritual heights where you will glimpse the glory of God's pain for humanity.

"Become a spiritual warrior and take up the sword of truth and light. By your deeds you will be known, and by your love you will be blessed."

12

♣ ♣ ♣

The following is a dedication to the great Archangel Michael, who cleaves through the darkness with his flaming sword of light:

Oh Blessed Michael
Great Architect of the Sun,
Who workest out the will of the Father of the World.
Going forth in thy strength.
The Sword of Light cleaving the darkness
Thy heart a pure flame of Love strong and radiant
Thou bearest the light that is Christ
Into the dark places of the Earth.
Give us thy strength,
Gird upon us thine armour of light,
Enkindle in our hearts the pure flame of Love,
That we may go forth strong and radiant
Bearing with us the Light, which is Christ, into the dark
    places.

ORDERS OF ANGELS

There are three hierarchical orders of angels, each consisting of three choirs, making a total of nine choirs of angels, as follows:

THOSE CLOSEST TO THE THRONE OF GOD

THE SERAPHIM: The highest order is the Seraphim, who have purifying and illuminating powers and are depicted as having six wings and flames of fire around them. They surround the throne of God and balance the movement of the heavens. They eternally give praise – "Holy, Holy, Holy, is the Lord God of Hosts".

THE CHERUBIM: They have the power of knowledge and are the heavenly counselors. They are the Guardians of Light throughout the Cosmos.

THE THRONES: They also work as heavenly counselors under the Cherubim. They are shown as wheels of fire and are guardian angels of every Planet. They represent the divine in all life.

DIVINE PRIESTS / PRINCES OF THE COURT OF HEAVEN

THE DOMINIONS: These beings carry the sceptre and sword, which are symbolic of their majestic and divine power over all creation. They help to integrate the material and spiritual worlds.

THE VIRTUES: They assimilate the Will of God and enfold Mother Earth in divine and pure energies.

THE POWERS: They carry flaming swords to protect humanity. They help to anchor the light of God's divine plan for our Planet and bring to humanity the vision of unity with all creation.

THE MINISTERING ANGELS

THE PRINCIPALITIES: These beings are guardians of large groups like towns, cities and nations. They also watch over the leaders of the Angelic Hosts.

THE ARCHANGELS: These are beings of great light and love, who are leaders of the Angelic Hosts.

THE ANGELS: These are being of light who work under the Archangels assisting all areas of creation. They heal, illuminate, purify and transform. All we have to do is to invoke their help, and they are happy to be of service.

I feel very humble to have somehow acquired the nickname 'the angel lady'. Since opening up to this illustrious band of angelic beings, I have asked for their help in every avenue of my existence. When I leave my home I ask them to guard it. When I drive in our car I ask for their protection and when my cat Tawny goes for a walk near a busy road I send an angel with her. I also use angels to help with my emotional responses. For instance, if I feel negative about a certain situation then I will elect an angel for that circumstance, and invite that messenger of light to come to my assistance. If I am nervous about an event, which is looming in my life, then I will call for the Angel of Courage. On the following pages are a few of my angel friends, who wish to share their love and wisdom with you.

Angels await the call to be of service to you, so when the need arises just sit quietly and bring them into your consciousness. They are not allowed to interfere with your freewill, but you will find that the solutions to your problems will come more easily to mind. They will also help you to remember those words of surrender 'Not my will, but thine Oh Lord'. For many years I have been blessed with the companionship of Angels. I have worked and meditated with these glorious Lights from God, and several of them have given me short messages to be included within the pages of this book. I suggest that my readers sit in the stillness of their own meditations and also commune with the Angels.

AN ANGEL OF LOVE – who has a heart centre radiating pink and amethyst rays into the world. These angels work in harmony with the Archangel Haniel, the Lord Maitreya and the Lord Kuthumi. When we open our heart in unconditional love, one of these glorious Angels will enter our heart centre.

"I can only bring to you a small fraction of what I feel for the human race. If I asked you to experience the full force of what you call love, you would not be able to endure the radiant vibrations. When you eventually reach our level of perception you will understand. You are so used to a love limited by emotions that the full power of this vibration would awaken negative reactions, thereby achieving the opposite to unconditional love. You must understand that every atom of creation is held together by this energy; every plant, tree and flower. Each time that you look upon God's creation, you are enfolded by this love. You only have to open up your heart to become a part of this dance of joy.

"Do not strain with your mind to bring this quality into your life. Just tune in to our light and let it flow naturally into your heart centre. Once you join with us, the power of love will open many doors for you. We will show you the Kingdoms of Nature and the glory of the Universe. In your meditations we will help you to experience the golden rays of Venus and the glory which is Sirius. Every portion of the Universe will open up its heart to you. Life will take on a new

17

expectancy and you will indeed become a 'Traveler of Light' on the pathway of universal love. You will enter the heart of God and know the true meaning of Paradise on Earth."

Use the above message as a meditation, choosing a beautiful pink rose to hold against your heart centre. Experience the love contained within the words and let unconditional love flow out into the World. The Angels will absorb this glorious energy and direct it to where it is most needed.

Love is the key which will eradicate any fear or phobia, and I will illustrate this by my own story. From my childhood my one big fear was of spiders. One look at their hairy bodies and scuttling legs, would send me into convulsions of terror. A boyfriend once chased me with this symbol of horror, with the result that I had hysterics for the next half an hour. If there was one in the bathroom or in the bedroom, I didn't wash or go to sleep. I knew that this was an irrational fear and longed to rid myself of its grip. I tuned in to the Angels of Love and the Devas who enfold spiders and asked for help. I didn't have to wait long.

One Thursday morning I was sitting in my local hairdressers, relaxing under the dryer, when the lady next to me suddenly touched me on the arm. "Excuse me", she said in a loud voice, "Did you know that you have a spider on your leg?"

I looked down and clamped to my calf was the biggest, ugliest monster that you could ever imagine. He sat and regarded me with baleful malevolence. I screamed and shook my skirt, dislodging him onto the floor. Customers and assistants shrieked, whilst jumping onto the nearest chairs. It appeared that the whole world suffered from arachnophobia.

One young girl, a little more courageous than the rest, fetched a broom. The subject of all this mayhem was squatting under a small table and I realised, with dismay, that she was about to squash him. Without a thought, and to save this creature from annihilation, I scooped him up in my hands and ran out of the shop door. It was whilst I was releasing him onto the nearest bush, that the full realisation of what I had done, struck me. Without cringing, I had held the menace of my worst nightmares in my hands, and felt his hairy body and legs against my flesh.

I am a vegetarian, and cannot abide the killing of any living creature. Love and compassion had overcome my terrible aversion and from that day onwards my deep-rooted fear left me. Spiders have become a part of God's loving kingdom, to be liked and respected. I now have no difficulty in living side by side with them. They spin their webs in various corners of my flat, knowing that they will be undisturbed.

AN ANGEL OF HEALING – who has a heart centre radiating all the colours of the spectrum into the world. These angels are in harmony with the Archangel Raphael and the Master Jesus. They pour their healing love through every atom of mans' body

> "We work very closely with the Angels of Love, as no healing would be possible without bringing the energy of love into the heart centre. We draw close to every hospital, healing clinic and sick room. We also work within veterinary clinic surgeries and wherever there is a sick animal.

> "We combine with the elementals who work on your physical frame. Each cell of your body has its own entity, endeavouring to bring balance to the chemicals, which flow through that particular cell. We try very

hard to draw the beauty of the light from your own soul into your body, as we wish to instill healing of both mind and spirit. When you invoke healing angels, we seek to create, within your consciousness, an understanding of the problems, which have caused your disease. When we work through spiritual healers, we pour God's energy into their hearts and out through their hands into the patient's etheric and physical bodies.

"Angels come from other parts of the Universe to witness the healing which is carried out on Mother Earth. There are other planets, far out in the realms of space, who need this skill. Many of you think that your planet is dark and dense. I can assure you that there are other worlds that vibrate at a much lower frequency than Earth. These are globes that cannot yet acknowledge the existence of Love, and this is where we need your help. A portion of every thought of healing love sent out by you eventually reaches these darker globes. Your love enfolds the soul of these planets bringing the first glimmer of light onto their surfaces. For this we bless you and thank you. Your Universe is still growing and expanding, and will eventually become the heart centre for a far greater entity of which you can have no knowledge at this present time."

"When you are in need of healing for yourself, or somebody else, ask that the Archangel Raphael and the Healing Angels draw close to you. Feel their energy pouring through your body and enfolding you. Relax and be at peace, letting the balm of their healing light bring you comfort and restoration."

Whilst working as a channel for God's healing energy, I have always asked for the assistance of Archangel Raphael and the Healing Angels. Through my studies of the Ancient Wisdom, I became aware of the spiritual power and beauty that is contained within a triangle. For instance, Father, Son and Holy Ghost; Wisdom, Love and Power. Several years ago, I was given the vision of two healing triangles linked together to form a six-pointed star. This is as ancient symbol of humanity, and as such, is of enormous benefit when applied to a sick patient.

This can be done whilst meditating, using visualisation to bring absent healing to the sufferer, or when giving contact healing for any ailment. I would also add that the six pointed star is held in deference and esteem within the White Eagle Lodge.

I visualise Archangel Raphael, Healing Angels and Master Jesus at the three tips of the triangle pointing downwards from God, with myself, my patient and the dis-ease pointing upwards towards our creator, as follows:

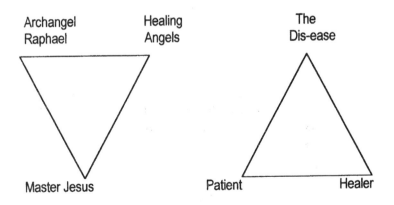

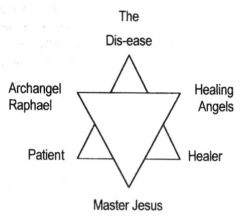

The
Dis-ease

Archangel
Raphael

Healing
Angels

Patient

Healer

Master Jesus

I always ask that the divine healing energy may pour through the star onto the dis-eased area of the patients body. I use my mind to bring forth the image and my heart to circulate the healing force. Before giving spiritual healing I stand behind my patient and visualise these sacred triangles with the healing energy flowing onto their body. I then apply contact healing in the normal way. Patients often tell me that whilst the healing was being given they perceived Angels and colours with their inner vision.

I have been asked if any damage can occur through the use of this symbol. My answer is that where there is genuine love pouring from the heart, there can be no danger to any form of life. Triangles can be used to bring healing to animals, plants, the Earth and even the Universe itself.

AN ANGEL OF PEACE – who has a heart centre radiating deep blue and gold. These angels work with the Archangel Michael and the Master Saint Germaine. They await the call from the compassionate hearts and minds of man.

"We have difficulty opening up your consciousness to the perception of deep peace. The human mind is so active that it cannot keep still long enough to experience even a small fragment of this divine energy. To rest in peace, is to enfold your whole body in a gentle, but mighty, cloak of calm. It has no beginning, and no end, only the infinite NOW. Within this peace there is no strain or stress; these emotions have been left at the feet of God. All passion has been stilled. All is forgiveness. All is acceptance. All is truth.

"We would like to take the whole of mankind in our arms, if you would let us. We wish to awaken within humanity a realisation of how your world will be when all strife has ceased, and there is only peace and harmony. You fear that it might become a boring vacuum, but we can assure you that it will be vibrant. There will be complete unity within all creation, where every one of you will be a part of each other. This equilibrium will spread its wings out into the Cosmos. Your Planet will become sacred, and will join the rolls of honour on which are inscribed the names of other Worlds of Light throughout the Universe.

"Your Solar system is very quickly raising in vibration and the Angels of Love, Healing and Peace will soon be your constant companions. We will open up your vision to realms of light beyond your present imagination. The word INFINITY will become a reality, and the phrase 'The Peace which Passeth all Understanding' will be within your grasp."

23

Relax in your favourite chair or under a well loved tree and let the Angel of Peace dwell within you. You are encircled in the colours of deep blue and gold. Bring into your inner vision a picture of our World as described by the Angel of Peace. Know this to be a reality deep within your heart, and bless all mankind wherever they may be. Your own body responds to these vibrations of peace, and you will return to your physical life refreshed and renewed.

AN ANGEL OF POWER – who has a heart centre radiating gold, orange and magenta. These angels work for the Archangel Metatron and the Master El Moya. They await the call from hearts and minds of man.

"Many of you have seen us with swords of flame as we join forces with the Angels of Peace and the Archangel Michael and his company of shining warriors Darkness will dissolve before our might, as we do battle with the thought forms which surround your earth. We unite with the Angels of the Earth, Air, Fire and Water to ease the pollution and destruction, which is afflicting your beloved globe. Within the etheric body of your earth are sacred centres, which are aligned with other planets in your solar system. We endeavour to balance the energies, which flow into these chakras, but this is not an easy task at your present stage of evolution. We labour very hard to impart fresh ideas into your higher minds, in order to bring about the restoration of your planet. The evolved people of your earth feel our presence, and it is to them that we turn our attention. We try to instill in their consciousness new concepts, on which you call 'green issues'. The mighty Solar Angels come to our aid in an endeavour to clear and transform the mists of poisonous gases which are rending asunder the protective layers around your globe.

"We have always stayed by the side of humanity, from the very start of your journey into matter. We were the Angels who lit up the skies in your ancient manuscripts, and hovered over France during the first and second world wars. Together with the Angels of Light, we try to clear the pandemonium and mayhem which hold mankind in its sway."

Join with the Angels of Power in your meditations, and allow their presence to bring strength to your spiritual and physical bodies. In your prayers ask that the Grace of God may fall upon our beloved Mother Earth. Hand in hand with these Angels, we will walk together into the dawning light of the coming Age, where the glory of Ascension awaits all humanity.

AN ANGEL OF WISDOM – who has a heart centre radiating violet and magenta rays. These angels are in harmony with the Archangel Uriel and the Lord Buddha. They await the call from the throats and minds of man.

"With wisdom comes freedom, and we work to bring to humanity the blessings of the intellect tempered with unconditional love. True wisdom unites the higher mind with the heart and has nothing to do with the earthly lower mind.

25

"True wisdom dissolves all fear. We join with the Angels of Hope to bring fortitude to the inhabitants of Earth. Fear encases your globe like a steel magnet. It draws towards itself all the other negative emotions of anger, greed, cruelty and resentment. We work to dispel this darkness and to draw humanity up into the realms of light. When heart and head are fully aligned, mankind will reach perfection, together with that great entity which you know of as GAIA, your beloved Mother Earth.

"Your planet is surrounded by visitors from other parts of the Universe. They are mostly within the etheric field of your globe, as to reveal themselves physically would create fear and misunderstanding. They await the dawn of what you call 'The Golden Age', so that they can help and celebrate with you the onset of a time of peace, illumination and spiritual wisdom. When humanity has done the ground-work, they will eventually share their knowledge with you, so that your higher minds may expand and mature. When this occurs, your inner vision will bring to earth manifestations and inventions far superior to anything that you dream of today. This knowledge will not be kept secret under lock and key. All nations will share and there will be no such thing as a third world. All people and countries will be equal, with the same opportunities. The light of early Atlantis will shine again on your planet, but at a far higher level of evolution. When the time is right, you will see these visitors from other worlds, who will bring with them their own angelic hosts and their own Masters of Wisdom. Look into the skies and bid them welcome."

With your inner vision see clearly these Angels of Wisdom. Welcome them into your hearts and minds. Allow them to work on the expansion of your knowledge.

Let them guide you into the Halls of Wisdom in your sleep, and bring back into your waking hours the enlightenment, which is stored in the collective consciousness of the Mind of your Creator.

AN ANGEL OF THE SUN – who has a heart centre radiating gold and the pure white light of Christ. These angels work closely with Universal Archangels, who draw close to earth to help in the evolution of mankind. They await the call from the minds of men.

"We pour the light of Christ down upon humanity from the spiritual sun, which lies behind your physical sun. We bring blessings to all creation on Mother Earth from the heart of God. We radiate love into the darkest crevices of your world, as we strive to illuminate all of physical matter, drawing out pain and anguish. The

God of this Universe is fully aware of every agonising tremor, which shakes any part of his kingdom. He seeks to alleviate this suffering by sending his angels to bring gentle healing and succour to his children.

"You do not realise how much you are loved and that each one of you is held within your Creator's heart. When you understand the words 'I AM', then you will comprehend that you are a small part of that great heart, and that you must learn to beat in harmony with that sacred expression of all life. Then you will know ecstasy and joy, which has nothing to do with the selfishness of conditional love which is practiced on your earth plane. You will begin to glimpse the freedom of the Universe, which awaits all of mankind. Open up your arms to the glory of the spiritual sun and let the angels of the Sun enfold and radiate the light into you chakra system. We ask you to give service from your hearts and know the true meaning of those blessed words 'I AM THE LIGHT OF THE WORLD'."

For a few moments each day visualise these glorious Angels of the Sun and allow them to pour their golden light of love through your crown centre. Feel this illuminating light filling every chakra and every cell of your body with spiritual sunlight. Bring this brilliance into your heart centre, allowing it to flow out to every part of creation on our beloved Mother Earth and into the Universe beyond.

AN ANGEL OF ASCENSION – who has a heart centre that radiates the beauty of the mother-of-pearl ray, which contains all the colours of the spectrum. This divine angel will help you to continually live within your higher self, until every cell of your physical body begins to vibrate at a higher frequency and becomes pure light. THIS IS THE GLORY OF ASCENSION.

"Dear Brothers and Sisters of the Light, as you read these words please realise that you are all light workers and guardians of Mother Earth. Now is the time to awaken and take up the torch, which will illumine your pathway to Ascension. The great Archangels of Universal Unconditional Love have anchored very powerful energies into your planet, thus slowly raising your consciousness to a higher frequency. Allow these purifying rays to pour through your bodies, transforming your cells into evolving atoms of Christ light. See yourselves enfolded in the glorious colours of violet, magenta and gold. Know that you are being revitalised and that these powerful vibrations will cleanse away all pollution from your bodies and the planet. From this day forth you will become beings of PURE UNCONDITIONAL LOVE. You will remember that this was the only quality which you brought to this planet from your Creator, and that it is this illuminated gift which you have agreed to share with all creation. Just by standing and radiating this unconditional love, you will increase the light vibrations within this Globe, and very soon the whole Earth will enter a new dimension and the golden age of Aquarius will be made manifest. Know that you are becoming limitless beings who can achieve any goal which is set for you."

Make yourself comfortable in your favourite chair and see before you a pathway of golden light. An Angel of Ascension is behind you and is enfolding you in wings of shining radiance. You are being drawn towards a horizon filled by a deep blue sky. As you walk toward the glory of spiritual brilliance. You look upon a face that is very familiar, and realise that you are gazing at the glory of your higher self. This sacred form stretches out a hand and gently guides you towards a Temple of Light. This is the Temple of Ascension; a place you can return to again and again in your search for illumination. This glorious being leads you to a crystal chair and sits besides you. You may like to converse with your higher self, asking questions with regard to your progress on the spiritual path. The more times that you contact your higher self, the quicker you will become united with your body of light – a perfected and illuminated human being.

The time has come for you to leave. Give thanks and blessings before you walk out of the temple and into a glorious sunny day. You now return to your familiar surroundings, encircled in a cloak of protection provided for you by your own special Angel of Ascension.

AN ANGEL OF COURAGE

"Every part of your planet needs fortitude and every cell of your body requires stalwart determination to continue on the path of life. Each hour of your day brings fresh challenges for you to meet and resolve. When you draw Angels of Courage into your presence, we will try to assist you to overcome these small and large initiations. We will bring before you a vision, which will allow you to review the road ahead. When your solar plexus is fluttering like a trapped moth, then we will calm and soothe your ruffled vibrations. We will help you to accept these struggles with love and fearlessness. Use the affirmation 'I AM DIVINE COURAGE AND I WILL NOT SUFFER' often throughout the day, until you feel peace and harmony returning to your physical existence. At the beginning of each new day, welcome these tests and trials both negative and positive, as a means by which your soul and spirit will grow strong in the service of the forces of light. Become aware of our closeness and allow the essence of our courage to enfold you with strength and boldness."

AN ANGEL OF FORGIVENESS

"Never forget that you continually dwell in the mind and heart of God. Our Creator is all forgiveness and knows your every failure and every fault. The great Masters of Light and Wisdom have trodden the path which you follow. They know every ordeal and tribulation that afflicts you and they watch over you with sympathy and understanding. We, the Angels of Forgiveness are their helpers and we work to bring light into your souls and spirits. In this way we can help you to reach self-absolution. In showing mercy to ourselves, you are forgiving all the defects and inadequacies which burden the minds of your fellow men.

"You perceive yourselves to be blemished, when in fact your hearts are awakening to the beauty of love and compassion. When you feel betrayed by another let the energy of forgiveness flow out to that person. You will then find that the same energy is working within you, breaking up old blockages and allowing the ice of resentment to melt into a pool of liberation. Use often the affirmation 'I FORGIVE MYSELF, I FORGIVE YOU, AND I SURROUND YOU WITH LOVING THOUGHTS'".

AN ANGEL OF ABUNDANCE

"We not only draw towards you plentitude, but also sustenance, both physical and spiritual. When you unite with the angelic realm, you are creating for yourselves the power to transmute and transform the energy of abundance. The Law of providence will provide you with all that you require to serve God and his creatures. You are loved and succoured and when you ask the Angels of Abundance for material help, this is often granted and sent to you with divine gladness. Soon all countries of the World will hold the key to abundance and there will no longer be starvation and famine. The Law of Sharing will hold sway and 'as you give, so shall you receive' will be understood by all men.

"The energy of abundance is not in any way related to wealth or riches. Always remember to count your blessings, in the knowledge that you have many gifts from spirit which vastly outweigh all material cravings. Go for a walk and look around you at the wealth of nature. This has no monetary value and its beauty is there for all humanity to partake of and enjoy. Let your thoughts dwell on the freedom of sharing which has nothing to do with the ownership of land or boundaries. When this earth is at last used for the common good of all people, then the Angels of Abundance will once more walk your paths and lands. We will unlock your chains of material imprisonment and throw away the keys of monetary desire."

AN ANGEL OF TENDERNESS

"We come to you on wings of gentleness and devotion. You will see us within every bud, every new leaf, every newly hatched bird and every newborn animal and child. We live within your deepest compassion and are rooted in your innermost vulnerability.

"We offer you a path of simple joy and a road of humble trust. Know, without doubt, that all is working out for the implementation of God's great plan on earth.

"We will help you to learn tolerance and forbearance. Always treat another person's views with benevolence, knowing that truth is contained within his words, even though they may differ from your own ideas. Be tender with yourselves, trusting in your own clear inner wisdom in times of trials. Learn of the humane-ness of the Angels of Tenderness, knowing that you are all enfolded in the love of spirit. Talk with your angelic helpers and messengers who are only waiting to serve you with gentleness and affection. The Master Jesus used tenderness, not as a sign of weakness, but as an instrument of love and strength. Even from the agony of the cross, he showed consideration and mercy to his torturers. Walk out into your lives with this tool of compassion and the angels will gather round and bless you. Your battle-cry will be love and your armour will be the shield of patience."

AN ANGEL OF CREATIVITY

"Without creative expression your world would cease to exist. The Angels of Creativity communicate thoughts of encouragement and inspiration. Every thought of beauty held within your mind creates a picture on the mental planes. It is then used to build a paradise on your physical earth.

"When you bring the Angels of Creativity into your lives, you will start to experience inspirational ideas. This does not mean that you have to write a bestseller, or paint a masterpiece. You can plant a glorious garden or create a home, which is a haven of love for your friends and family. In fact you can begin to establish a world filled with positive and beneficial ideas. Thoughts are units of energy and can be used to stimulate joy and harmony. The Angels of Creativity will gather around you, helping to initiate all the constructive emotions, which are building within your higher mind. They will, for instance, assist you to achieve self-worth, independence, integrity, generosity and faith. They will bring colour into your existence and help you to work with the positive essences of each shade. They will also aid you in your meditations, so that you will create imaginative visions, which will swiftly become reality.

"These positive exercises will enable you to unblock many restrictions, and allow the energies to flow blissfully through your chakra system. Experience again the joy of being a child. Learn once more how to play, laugh and dance. Creativity will allow innocence and purity to enter your consciousness. You will realise that you are indeed a child of God clothed in a material body.

"Let happiness fill your life and permit freedom of spirit to arrive as a result of your own creative thoughts".

YOUR GUARDIAN ANGEL – is an angel who is with you at all times and on every level of consciousness.

"We are not only guardians of humanity, but also of countries, groups and establishments. We love you all dearly, and await with joy the moment when you are ready to acknowledge our presence. Then we have a jubilant celebration in the world of light, which echoes to the sound of our grateful thanks to God for the awakening of your inner vision and recognition of our existence.

"Once you accept our company, we are better able to guide and inspire your life into avenues of learning and service. We do not in any way interfere with your freewill and are not allowed to intrude upon your karma. We are always there, however, to encourage and cheer you on. We would never abandon you, however negative the situation which surrounds you becomes. We have been with you for thousands of years, and will walk with you for quite a few thousand more. The spiral of evolution is so exact that it is only through contact with humanity that our own progression can occur.

"Know that we are your best friends, your partners on the path of light. We bring into your consciousness wise teachers and angels from the higher planes. When the time is ripe we will even guide you out into the universe and beyond, allowing you glimpses of the great angels who supervise the evolution of our solar system. We are divine expressions of God who wait to serve you, and lovingly help you to transform your hearts and minds into vehicles of light."

One of the first angels that I became aware of during meditation was my Guardian Angel. I was meditating on a pure white candle, watching the flame begin to grow larger and larger, when I became aware that the candle and its glow had become a form of pure golden light. The form wrapped its wings of light, pure streams of loving energy, around me, giving me a sense of perfect peace, a feeling of great calmness. I asked this being who he was, although I already knew the answer within my soul. Since then I have felt the presence of my Guardian Angel many times and I know he is always there, waiting to help if it was within his power.

There have been two instances when I have really needed this Angel's help. The first happened several years ago when I had arranged to give a series of short afternoon lectures in a local hall. I was about to commence the first talk, when the door opened to allow three people to enter and take their seats in the second row. It was an introductory address, about the many spiritual aspects awaiting a disciple on the path of light. For the first five minutes all went well, until I became aware that I was having difficulty remembering what came next.

I began to panic, as I use very few notes and normally rely on what is channeled into my brain. To gain a breathing space, I gave the audience a chance to study their diagrams and examine the blackboard. Quickly I tuned in to the energies circulating around the room.

Everything I encountered was positive until I reached the three latecomers in the second row. Their auras were emanating a very negative vibration; especially from one of them, a black haired strong looking character who was obviously their leader. The force they were using was blocking my thought patterns, making it impossible for me to bring forth my usual flow of words. Quickly I sealed myself with light, calling on my Guardian Angel, the Angels of Love and the Angels of Power.

From my heart centre I sent a beam of love to surround and enfold my three adversaries. By the time I resumed my lecture the atmosphere had lightened, and I found that everything was practically back to normal. Realising what was occurring, the three very grey practitioners waited until a coffee break and then left. I do not know what their motive was. Could it have been envy or jealousy? Could it have been an exercise in power? Or was it darkness trying to overthrow light? Whatever the reason, the Angelic Hosts of Guidance and Love had once more triumphed. There is nothing in this world or the next that can stand against the force of unconditional love.

The second instance occurred recently, during my stay in Perth, Western Australia. I was attending a late evening meeting and my beloved friend with whom I was staying, gave me a spare key to let myself into her house. I arrived home at midnight and tried the key in the lock. Horror – nothing happened, the key refused to turn and the door would not open. I had been given the wrong key. My hostess was fast asleep and despite much banging, ringing and shouting, I failed to wake her.

After much thought I decided that the only solution was to find a telephone and ring her. I saw a neighbour's light was on and tapped on her window. A very timid woman's face appeared. She was too afraid to open the window, but informed me that there was a telephone box four blocks down the road.

It was now 12.30 a.m., on a very dark and cloudy night. I was carrying my handbag and wearing very bright colours that showed up against the yellow street lights. As I walked, I became aware of the headlights of a car following me. A black sleek vehicle drew up alongside me and was about to stop. I knew that I needed help, and summoned my Guardian Angel and again the Archangel Michael. I surrounded myself in a circle of golden light and sent unconditional love from my heart to the impending danger. After what seemed like hours, but could only have been a few seconds, I heard the car draw away from the curb and quickly speed into the distance.

I now felt completely safe and protected by the Angelic realm. I found the telephone box, managed to awaken my friend and returned safely to her home. She welcomed me with much love and concern, and after a strong cup of coffee I went happily to bed.

I would ask all my readers to tune into the essence of the angelic realm. Talk to your own Guardian Angels and let them bring to you the beauty of God's love, truth and understanding. Allow them to open up the door onto the spiritual planes so that the Garden of Eden will once more blossom on earth, and all of Gods creatures will live in light and love.

One of the most beautiful angels that I have ever seen with my physical eyes, was the Angel of Death. I was giving healing to a friend's husband who was very seriously ill. In fact it was the day before he passed over into the light. I became aware of a change of vibration within the room. I looked towards the corner near to his bed, and saw a shape of pure white light forming. It became so bright that I knew that I mustn't look directly at it or I would be blinded. Within my mind I heard the words 'I am waiting to take him, when you have finished'. How could I ever be frightened of dying, when a being of such love and compassion awaits my passing? To be held in his arms would be to experience the moment of death as touching the lips of God. No more pain, no more fear just pure ecstasy and rebirth into our rightful home in the realms of light.

To end the Angel section of this book, I am including a beautiful poem entitled 'Contemplation', which was composed by a very dear friend of mine, Joan Fugeman.

You may wish to use this as a meditation, bringing into your vision the Angels who work with the Earth, Air, Fire and Water. Reflect on the meaning of the inspired words, and picture yourself as a joyous part of creation.

CONTEMPLATION

I AM

I AM the simple grain of sand
That moves within this checkerboard of day and night.
A traveler on the arduous path
that leads the way from darkness into light.

I AM the feathery seed of a dandelion clock,
Blown by the winds of heaven to rest afar
In the crevice of a distant rock.

I AM a droplet of the ocean's tide,
That flows through stream and river
To return once more from whence it came
To where it must abide.

I AM the joy in the nightingale's song
In the still evening, heard through the night long,
The sheer delight in the heart of a bird,
who calls to his mate,
And can do no wrong.

I AM the love that flows around the world,
In every tree and flower unfurled,
In animal life stream near and far,
From the lowly insect to furthest star.

I AM peace in the sunset's evening glow,
In the quiet stillness of breaking dawn,
Where streams of living water flow
And the dew on a rosebud in early morn.

I AM the colour in nature that brings
The radiant hue to a butterfly's wings.
The golden splendour of Autumn's fall,
The crimson foliage on a garden wall.

I AM ALL THAT I AM
With all life forms,
In tranquil sea, in turbulent storms,
I AM ONE with the UNIVERSAL MIND
The Light in the Heart of Humankind.

Joan Fugeman.

Section Two

NATURE SPIRITS OF TREES AND FLOWERS

THE NATURE SPIRITS OF TREES AND FLOWERS

THE TREES
(A Portuguese Prayer)

You who pass by and raise a hand against
us, heed well our prayer before you harm us.

We are fuel for your fires on cold nights,
the friendly shade protecting your form the
fierce sun, and our fruits are refreshing
to quench your thirst and cheer you as you
journey on.

We are the rafters of your roofs, the bodies
of your boats, the seats of your stools, and
the boards of your beds.

We are the handles of your hoes, the gates of
your homes, the wood of your cradles and the
shells of your coffins.

We are the saviours of your soil from loss
by rain and winds, and to your soil we give
richness and life for the benefit of all men.

We are the bread of kindness and the flowers of
beauty.

Ye who pass by listen to our prayer and harm
us not.

This beautiful incantation expresses the balance throughout nature, which is a perfect thought of God. Everything has its place within the divine inspiration of the great architect who uses our Universe as an expression of his physical body.

For millions of years this equilibrium held sway on our planet, until man decided that he was superior to his God and chose to upset the balance for personal gain and the accumulation of great riches. In just one hundred years we have managed to rape the earth of its mineral resources and destroy vast areas of forest and fauna. We have torn down our rain forests and woods in the ceaseless pursuit of raw materials for paper and commercial wealth. Every time a ton of advertising material lands on our doormats, thousands of living trees have died, together with the nature spirits and animals who inhabit them.

Man has also managed to weaken the remaining trees to such an extent that they are falling victim to disease and acid rain. We now see on our television screens the horror of forest fires, annihilating huge areas of woodland in many parts of the world. The very soil which produces nutrients to feed the plants has been poisoned by chemical fertilizers and industrial waste. This whole scenario is a tragedy not only for the plant kingdom, but for animals, man and the nature spirits. The trees are the lungs of our planet and the delicate interchange between oxygen and carbon dioxide has been disrupted adding to the serious greenhouse effect. We have all become aware of the changes to our climate with desert conditions in some countries and excessive rainfall in others.

Slowly, and thankfully, this situation is changing as man becomes aware of the dangers to himself and the earth. We see many lifesaving schemes being organised, from the banning of certain chemicals to the planting of millions of new trees all over our globe. The word 'organic' has become fashionable, thus allowing the worms and natural minerals to return to the soil. With the reinstatement of the forests and woodlands will come the reappearance of large numbers of tree devas and nature spirits, who work on the etheric bodies of the trees to succour and nurture the young saplings.

There have always been ancient legends, which tell about the wisdom of the trees. In many old civilisations they were worshipped for their power and discernment. The Celts talk of the 'Tree of Knowledge' whilst the Kabbalists have always seen the 'Tree of Life' as a symbol of spiritual balance between negative and positive. Buddha received enlightenment under the Bodhi tree. Odin hung from a tree, whilst the Lord Jesus was crucified on a cross of wood. Trees are the high initiates of the plant evolution and if we will allow their energy to flow through our bodies, they will help us to travel along our own path to enlightenment.

I recall walking in a park one day and passing through a magnificent avenue of trees. Suddenly, I became totally conscious of my unity with all life. I knew that the trees were my brothers and that the animals and birds were as much my family as were my own relatives. I also perceived that every act of goodness was a part of my awareness, just as every act of evil had its effects of my consciousness. The energy, we call God, pervades every atom on this earth, uniting all creation within his power of pure love. This realisation will eventually lead us back to complete union within the heart centre of our Creator.

As a small child I was able to see little lights within trees and bushes, which I later realised were nature spirits. I feel that most children can see these, but the ability leaves them when they are told by well meaning adults that they

46

have an over-active imagination. People often ask me "How can we see the gnomes, elves and pixies who inhabit the trees?" My advice is to go into the centre of a wood, sit very still and tune into the beauty of nature. Look deep into the leaves and bushes and you may begin to perceive a slight movement where there is no breeze. A feather may fall at your feet, or a gentle touch on your cheek, like cobwebs, will indicate the presence of Nature Spirits. Look at shapes on the trunks and branches of trees, and again you will begin to perceive the forms of pixies and elves. In your meditations see these small beings of light, and they will soon become a reality within your physical existence.

The voice of God echoes through all creation and the nearest that I have ever been to hearing this intonation, was on a visit to the home of my dear friend Joan Fugeman. She lives in the centre of a wood of ancient origin. To say that it is enchanted would be an understatement, as it is filled with the essence of nature spirits and tree devas. Whilst I was there, Joan took me for a walk through these woods to make the acquaintance of her 'bee tree'. Previously she had told me how she had meditated with her back to the trunk and suddenly found that she was enfolded in the sound of the AUM. This reverberation seem to be all around her, and within her. When she opened her eyes she discovered that she was engulfed in small brown bees. They did no harm, as they had felt her great love for all of God's creatures. The bees had made their home in a hollow between the roots of this magnificent beech tree.

I was very eager to make their acquaintance, so I quietly stood with my back to the tree and poured out my love to these remarkable insects. Within seconds they were gently swarming up my legs, my body, my arms, around my face and my head. I felt that they had accepted me as their friend and were echoing the glorious sound of the

AUM for me. It rose and fell like the sighing of the wind. It appeared to fill all time and space with its grandeur. It was as old as the Universe, yet as young as the smallest seed. It was truly a reflection of the voice of God at the dawn of creation.

After a while I left the beech tree. The bees followed me for a short distance and then returned to their busy work within the peaceful haven of the roots. It was a sad fact that most of these woods, and this monumental beech, were due for demolition. We have a huge traffic problem in England, and we are very short of roads, so Joan's beautiful woods were doomed to become part of a freeway. Gone would have been the serenity, giving way to the roar of traffic and the odour of diesel fumes wafting over the remaining shrubbery.

Joan, who has great faith, went one day to the woods and contacted the Deva of the beech tree, hoping that some miracle might save its wonderful boughs and branches. In order to remember this part of the woods, she took several photographs. When we looked at the pictures of the beech tree an awesome sight appeared before our eyes. We could clearly see the shape of nature spirits within its foliage. The angelic realm were showing themselves to Joan in recognition of her love and compassion for their forest home.

There is, however, a happy ending to this story. England is also very short of money and the local government ran out of funds, as did the Contractor who was building the freeway. Quite a number of Joan's friends had meditated on this problem, and I feel that the great Archangel who is the Guardian of these Woods had intervened at a higher level. There are no plans, in the future, to continue the construction of this freeway. When we join forces with the angelic realm, miracles do indeed occur.

I always see tree devas as orbs of glowing light, surrounding and stretching up beyond the highest branches. Their vibrant brilliance is matched only by the colours of nature that flow from their heart centres. To begin to perceive these great tree devas, I would suggest to my readers, that you find a large tree and stand back from it so that you can see the whole trunk and branches outlined against the sky. Close your eyes a little so that you are squinting or looking out through the slits of your eyes. Gaze at the top of the tree and you should begin to see a faint halo of light over the treetops. This is the beginning of the etheric form of the tree deva. You may also perceive the presence of nature spirits, who always appear to me as small flashes of light which dart and flit around the leaves, flowers and plants. If you place your hands on the trunk of a tree you can feel the heartbeat of this evolved life force, and gain strength and vitality from this connection.

I have discovered that the energy of trees can be either 'male' or 'female'. If when you place your hands on the trunk the energy appears to flow upwards towards the sky, then that is a male vibration. If, however, it flows downwards into the earth, then that power is female. The trees delight in communing with us, and within the following pages I will share with you some of their teachings. It is also possible to obtain the same result by holding a picture of a tree or flower during meditation, and letting the love from your heart link with the appropriate nature spirit. I would urge my readers to experience the beauty of this contact for themselves, and you will be amazed at the outcome. When love and faith flow between all forms of life, it is possible to give and receive from the smallest blade of grass to the farthest star. The energies from the trees, planets, and flowers can be of enormous benefit to our whole system, their healing properties acting on specific ailments within our physical bodies. There are many perfumed oils and incense sticks, which carry the scent of individual flowers and shrubs. When used within our homes, they can ensure that a relaxed and positive atmosphere prevails.

I have already mentioned that as a child I could perceive tiny lights in trees and bushes, which were the presence of Nature Spirits. As I progressed on my healing path, I became more and more able to see them with my physical eyes. I was quietly sitting by a river when I had my first physical sighting of a Nature Spirit. What I thought was a clump of thistledown floated into my vision. Suddenly, with a grasp of delight, I realised that what I was looking at was not thistledown, but the form of a small Fairy, complete with tiny wings, legs and arms. There was an equal look of surprise on her face as she recognised that I could also see her. She increased her speed and vanished into a nearby leafy tree. Since then I have seen elves and pixies and other denizens of the Nature realm. It normally happens when I least expect it, and quite often when I am not even thinking about Nature Spirits.

These delightful little manifestations from God will come into your homes if you will let them. They love flowers, plants, peace and harmony. It is said that trolls and gnomes love the dark of attics or the damp of basements. I can remember as a child, going into a friend's basement and knowing that something was watching me. The hairs on the back of my neck stood up, and as I turned I had the clear impression of a small dark shape about 3 ft high. It scuttled away quickly into a gloomier part of the basement, as I myself left in some haste. They are never threatening, but inquisitive and questioning.

Now is the time to again welcome these tiny sparks of creation as friends and helpers. Whenever there is a task to perform, be it in house or garden, ask them to assist you. You may not want to scrub a floor or do some weeding, but with their help it will become interesting and will not take nearly so long. I am a busy lady and I know that they aid me with my housework. However, I was very pleased to hear a Lecturer on Nature Spirits say that they liked a bit of dust. They probably think that my home is paradise!!!

Nature spirits can be called the Artist's Palette of God. They will enhance the colours and myriad variety of hues all over our earth. Without them, our Planet would lack brilliance and be a very drab place to inhabit. They have the ability to change and brighten any colour they touch with their essence.

I was taking an Angel Workshop recently, and wanted the participants to experience the energy of Tree Spirits. I had visited my Host's glorious garden early in the morning and asked the trees and shrubs if they would allow me to collect a few of their leaves. I also invited the Nature Spirits to transmit some of their energy into the leaves.

In the afternoon I asked all the people at the Workshop to pick a leaf and hold it between their hands. Everybody closed their eyes and for a few minutes tuned into the energy of the leaves. I knew that some would feel the energy and a few would bring into their inner vision the forms of elves and pixies etc. I was not at all prepared for what actually happened. When everybody had opened their eyes, I encouraged them to share any experiences. The lady who organised the Workshops was the first to speak. "It is very strange, but my leaf has gone all shiny". Someone from the back of the room hesitantly said "I wasn't going to mention it, but my leaf has changed colour. It was dark green and now it is much lighter." A man this time piped up "Tiny holes like eyes have appeared in mine." Yet another excited participant exclaimed "The top of my leaf has changed to light green!" A further lady said "I had two leaves joined together. They have now parted and one is a completely different shade of green to other."

That afternoon the Nature Spirits and the great Tree Devas who enfold clumps of trees, woods and gardens had decided to show us how they perform their work. They had combined their energy with our vibrations, to change the structure within the cells of the leaves. This, to them, was very simple. By allowing us to share this phenomenon, they had demonstrated a tiny aspect of what it means to be a Co-creator with God. As we continue to raise our vibrations, more of these natural abilities will be given to us.

The Nature Kingdom has favourite places where they congregate. They love the banks of streams and besides lakes and seashores. They will gather in hedgerows and in the cool glades of forests and woods. Look carefully as you walk between the trees, and you may come upon a fairy ring. Ask permission, and then stand within this circle. Several people have told tales of glimpsing the fairies dancing and being bewitched by their music.

I was in South Africa recently, at a place called the Hogg's Back. I had been asked to do a small evening talk in a magnificent garden, filled with many varieties of tree and bush. As I arrived I was greeted by a small girl who insisted on showing me where the fairies have their home.

This tiny child led me to a huge Yew Tree, and pointed to the image of an Archway that had formed naturally on the outside of its massive trunk. "That's where the fairies go." she said. "Do you see fairies?" I asked. "Oh yes" she retorted "They are my friends and they play with me." I thought how magical it was that this child would grow up with full understanding of all this enchantment which evolves alongside mankind.

This then is my quest into some of the spiritual aspects of trees and plants. There is a connection with these lifeforms, through the chakras within man's etheric body:

ASH – Blending with the Brow and Crown Centres

"Long ago I was known as 'The Tree of Life' I like to grow in the cool, clean air of mountains and hills, away from the contamination of towns and cities. My upper branches gaze upon the dawn of a new day and oncoming of night. I watch the fresh beauty of the sunrise and the thanksgiving of a sunset. I have seen the passing of time throughout the Universe and I have knowledge of events past and of experiences to come. Time has little meaning, as I can look into other dimensions and understand the great truth that there is only the immediate 'now'. Everything else is an illusion. I can bring to man a clear picture of the mental planes. I will encourage you to reach out with your minds to gather fresh ideas and concepts. This will inspire you both spiritually and creatively.

"I can commune with the sylphs of the air and read the messages on the winds of change. I will help to cool the fury of the elementals as they rage within a Winter's storm. My branches bend in a tempest but never break. My roots reach down into the coolness of the ground, seeking the rhythm of the earth. I AM LIFE, LIFE, LIFE."

MEDITATION

Place your hand on an ash tree, close your eyes and feel the energy of the tree unite with your body. The ash will bring you inner visions of dimensions yet to be revealed to humanity. Let your heart join with your mind to raise you into the higher mental levels. Draw towards yourself the sylphs and nymphs of the air and let them carry you into the realms of light. Here you will see forests and gardens filled with trees and plants as yet unknown on earth. As you come back from your meditation let your heart unite with the ash tree so that you become aware of the sanctity of all life. This will bring joy into your heart and peace into your mind.

BIRCH – In harmony with the Polar Plexus Centre.

"My branches and twigs are used to make brooms with which to sweep your floors free of dirt and grime. In this way I have become a symbol of humanity, and can help you to overcome any self-admiration from the ego. We, the trees, have also been planted on this earth to learn lessons. Many of us have been left besides motorways or in the middle of housing estates. We see the best and the worst in humanity. We view tragedies and yet also see the bravery of mankind. Battles have been fought around our trunks, resulting in the death of many people. We, too, have suffered. We have been torn from the earth by our roots, and felled to the ground to make way for what you call 'progress'. Yet we still love you and wish you to succeed. We see you pick yourselves up and try, try, again. In fact we see the glory of the future which lies ahead of you, if you will just stop and listen to your hearts. All will be well. I AM HOPE, HOPE, HOPE."

MEDITATION

When you are in conflict with yourself or another, find a Birch tree and sit with your back against its trunk. You will soon feel more at peace, and be able to find a solution to the contention. Listen to what your heart is telling you and not what your lower self would wish to hear. The negative of your nature would prefer to engage in discord rather than peace. Let the birch tree help to bring you back onto the pathway of light where only love and forgiveness hold sway. Push back the darkness and bring in the brightness and beauty of your own soul.

CEDAR – In balance with the Base and Crown Centre.

"The redness of my wood aligns me with the element of fire, so that I am aware of the Salamanders who inhabit the flames of nature. I can understand the emotions of fire, amongst which are anger, rage and fury. Yet my branches and leaves are also used for shade and protection in hot arid lands. In this way I work as an antidote, bringing the gentle breeze of temperance to any situation.

"The colour of my wood signifies courage and bravery. I can help you submit your personal will to the Will of God. My energy will assist you to transfer the fires of passion from your base centre to your crown chakra. In this way you can transmute your baser instincts into the true gold of spiritual attainment. I AM CALM, CALM, CALM."

MEDITATION

If you are feeling anger or resentment, find the shelter of a cedar tree and put your arms around its trunk. Breathe deeply, and slowly the fires which are burning within your lower chakras will ease and the bile you feel collecting in your throat will abate. You can then listen to the energy of the cedar tree as it cools and soothes. You are at peace, no more anger, no more distress, the raging fire has become the tiny glow of love within your heart.

CHESTNUT – In unity with the Brow and Crown Centre.

I have a favourite tree which I visit, quite near to where I live in Sussex. It is a huge spreading Chestnut, which gives me healing and strength. A great hurricane struck our County a few years ago, devastating and uprooting trees which had stood for hundreds of years. All night it raged, and when it was over the first thing I did was race as fast as I could to 'my tree'. There it stood in all its majesty, safe and serene – still a haven for my needs. This is what the chestnut tells me:

"You have been to me many times to place your hands on my bark and feel the energy flowing through my trunk. We have united, thus allowing the deva who gives me life to blend with the love from your heart. Whenever you are in need of healing or are depleted of energy I can assist you. Sometimes you may feel lost in the labyrinth of change and I can help you to draw on your inner resources. Never look back to what has passed, always look ahead to what is to come. I also represent the stability of 'now' and will open up a clear picture of this moment, which will never come again. Just as I am unique and you are unique, so is the moment you have just passed through. No one single person's moment is the same. Every atom on this planet experiences a different 'now', which is all part of the divine energy, which made me, you and the passing moment. I am still nonetheless, a part of you, just as you are a part of me and we are both a part of the moment that has now vanished. Stride into the future with courage, strength and confidence. I AM UNITY, UNITY, UNITY.

MEDITATION

I would like my readers to venture out and find their own tree. It doesn't have to be a chestnut, just any particular tree that seems to draw you towards it. As you meditate with this tree, you will soon begin to experience the interflow of energy. You may have to return to the same spot several times before it will speak to you. Use your inner vision to see the nature spirits who work within its structure. Sit and allow the woodland creatures to come to you without fear. Listen to the birdsong and smell the grasses and flowers which grow around its roots. Try and experience the whole activity of the tree, thus uniting with the magnificent deva whose lifeforce you are enjoying.

ELM – In harmony with the Heart Chakra.

"As I am the most sensitive of all the trees, I have been chosen to show humanity what will happen if he does not cease the pollution and destruction of the forests. I did not contract what you call 'Dutch Elm Disease' by chance. I was asked if I would sacrifice myself for the planet and humankind. Because of my love and compassion for you, I have allowed my physical body to know pain and distress, to feel my energy depleting and my sap ceasing to rise. Within my trunk is the smell of decay and death. Look on me with kindliness but do not weep too much, as my sacrifice is all part of my evolutionary path. The deva and nature spirits within my aura will benefit from this experience. We will all incarnate again together, in an age when man has ceased all strife and is ready to live side by side with his brothers, be they animal, vegetable, mineral or human. I AM SACRIFICE, SACRIFICE, SACRIFICE.

MEDITATION

In your reflections, change the pollution of this planet into a positive picture of restoration. See the world covered by forests and woodlands, which are pure and unspoilt. Imagine that large tracts of woods are set aside for the angels and nature spirits. Visualise the seas and rivers as clean and sparkling. See the whole earth surrounded by light, allowing the sunshine to pour down onto an undamaged planet.

OAK – Representative of the Base and Crown Centres

"I am the symbol of strength. My mighty roots sink deep into the soil and my outspread branches reach out to the farthest corners of the world. You will see my seed planted all around the globe, the vibrant young saplings springing up in field and glade. I have stood for hundreds of years in the shadow of castles and within sight of the humblest of dwellings. Do not limit me, however, to your realm of solid matter. I can reach up into the spiritual realms of light, where I also inhabit a body, giving you a glimpse of the continuation of all life. I can help you to understand eternity and bring to you the knowledge of past ages. The mistletoe, which sometimes grows around my trunk, will bring back to you memory of past rituals performed under my branches. The wind in my leaves will enable you to hear the music of the spheres and the song of sirens. I am aligned with the element of earth, so you will quickly be able to glimpse the darting light of nature spirits which shelter within my frame. I AM SPIRITUAL STRENGTH, STRENGTH, STRENGTH.

MEDITATION

Find the safety and comfort of a large oak tree. Sit with your back against the trunk and become aware of the rhythm of its breathing. Allow yourself to be lifted into the spheres of light, drifting on the wings of a gentle wind. Hear the music of the angels as they sing within the golden temples of invocation and healing. When you return to the protection of the oak tree send out your love to the deva of the tree. You may even be able to glimpse the figure of the 'green man' who guards this sacred oak. He will also be your friend and protect you from harm.

PINE – In accord with the Crown Centre

"We are the ears of the nature kingdom. We grow in large quantities all over the earth. We listen to the voices of man and we hear the despair and anguish as you speak. We listen and we understand your sorrow as we gaze upon the results of man's greed. We would counsel you, nonetheless, to send out positive thoughts into the world. Do not become negative with self-criticism. Value your inner self and let the love from your heart reflect your good intentions to your younger brethren. Share your love, my children of God, and you will find peace wherever you walk. Rest your hands on my trunk and I will bring you peace, free from struggle, and an acceptance of God's will on earth. I AM DIVINE ACCEPTANCE, ACCEPTANCE, ACCEP-TANCE

MEDITATION

With your inner vision imagine that you are standing between two very tall pine trees. The energies from both of these trees flow into your body, bringing balance and an awareness of all that you have achieved in this incarnation. You begin to realise how much you are loved and valued by your friends in spirit. Every act of kindness has been noticed and every positive thought that you have achieved has been written on the pages of time. Inhale the perfume of the pine needles into your body, allowing the purifying vapours to cleanse and refresh you.

SYCAMORE – In sympathy with the Throat Centre

"I am the messenger of the Gods. In ancient Egypt I was honoured because of my position at the entrance to the spiritual realms. My seeds are scattered across the face of the earth on the gentlest of breezes. I bring you joy and fun from the angels and the Masters who watch over mankind. Life should be lived with gleeful laughter and blissful delight. I dislike long and dismal faces. When you shelter under my canopy of leaves, let me see you smile. Count your blessings and let all the world see a happy being when you meet. Affirm that life is good, even allowing for the ups and downs of human existence. That is the message that I bring to you. Walk as tall as the highest tree and let the world delight in your joyfulness. I AM JOY, JOY, JOY.

MEDITATION

Picture yourself dancing and singing around a sycamore tree. Visualise yourself being lifted on the breezes of a summer's day and being scattered all over the earth on the wings of a sycamore pod. Imagine that you are planting love and joy throughout the planet, filling the earth with positive and beneficial thoughts. Look deep into the heart of man and see the goodness, which dwells within his soul. You are the instrument that will bring this to the surface every time you reflect on his virtues, surrounding his misdeeds with compassion and tenderness.

YEW – In balance with the Base and Crown Centre

"My lifespan of growth on your planet often stretches to a thousand years. I am mighty and I am strong. I am the tree of the mystics, because I stand between life and death. I am darkness and I am light. My berries are poisonous to eat, symbolising the bitter taste of negative action. My wood glows with colour and when polished displays areas of light and shade. I share all of your sins and all of your virtues.

In past ages I was the tree under which discussions and decisions were made. I am the judgement tree and this is why you will often find me growing in churchyards. If you will come and rest by my trunk I will assist you to reach important decisions. My energies will help you to see right from wrong and enable you to listen to what your conscience is telling you. I can aid you in becoming aware of your true inner self, that inner light which is the real and eternal you. I AM TRUTH, TRUTH, TRUTH.

MEDITATION

Only meditate under this tree if you wish to know the truth about yourself and a situation. You might not like what you see and the answer that you receive may not be what you wanted to hear. It will be candid and exact and will act as a mirror for your soul.

WILLOW – In complete harmony with the heart centre

"I am called the 'weeping willow' because I am able to cry for the sorrows of mankind. The depth of my compassion makes me an object of pure love, with which I can connect to the heart chakras of humanity and the great Universal heart of God. My love and sympathy enfolds all of creation as it struggles along the path of experiences. I grow near rivers and lakes so I am a friend to the Water Sprites, and my twigs are often used for water divining. The tips of my branches bend over and touch the ground, enabling me to attune to the heartbeat of Mother Earth. The sun's rays shine upon my bent head and radiate along my leaves, bringing to me the warmth of the Salamanders. I flourish in the winds and gales, so my love and understanding encompasses all the Sylphs of the Air. I AM LOVE, LOVE, LOVE."

MEDITATION

Stand, or imagine, that you are held within the flowing branches of a willow tree. Your heart centre opens with pure love for all creation. You meet with the Nature Spirits of the Earth, Air, Fire and Water. See yourself in the raindrops that fall from the sky and into a fast running stream. Flow with the waters of this river as it sinks deep into the soil. Become a part of a seed as it pushes itself through the earth and reaches towards the sky. Feel the sun shining down upon your body as you grow and progress on the pathway of life.

The plant kingdom holds within its leaves and flowers many properties which can balance and aid the human body. It is said that wherever there is disease, God gave us a plant that would act as an antidote. The closer we draw to the nature realm, the more we will discover about the spiritual attributes of plants. The following are just a few of the flowers that allowed me to contact the nature spirits which dwell within their leaves:

THE CARNATION – In sympathy with the Heart and Throat Centre

"I hold within my petals the essence of all life. We, whom you call the flowers, love the soil for its warmth and protection. Truly we are enfolded by mother earth and with gratitude we open our petals to the sun, our father. The bees who feed off our pollen are our brothers, and the moon that shines down on us at night is our sister. The raindrops refresh us, and the land on which we grow feeds us. We are all one. The remedial properties of the carnation are in the colours of their petals and the perfume that you inhale. Breathe in the splendour of our scent, and any depression or gloom will melt away. Choose any colour from our blooms, pick it and wear it on your person. Your day will then become filled with lightness and joy. This is the reason why we are always used as buttonholes for weddings. We spread love and devotion within the shades and perfume of our petals.

MEDITATION

With your inner vision behold a flowerbed of different coloured carnations. See the petals from these blooms floating away on a gentle breeze. You are now in the midst of a shower of colour, falling at your feet like a multi-shaded carpet. You are happy and contented; all your worries are forgotten; nothing can disturb your peace of mind. The nature spirits that live within the aura of the carnations are your friends, and weave a loom of colour around your physical frame. This will bring you healing and happiness in the days ahead.

THE GERANIUM – In balance with the Sacral and Solar Plexus Centres

"I am also a flower which will bring you cheerfulness and contentment. The nature spirits who inhabit my leaves and petals are always joyful. They are ever watchful for humans who have heart centres which radiate love. Grow me in your garden and the rest of the foliage will sing a song of bliss. My contentment flows through my leaves, allowing them to be used to heal many of humanities afflictions caused by imbalance and congestion. In particular I will work to regulate mans' reproductive cycles, helping him to understand the true glory of the sexual act of creation. I will help to lift depression and alleviate anxiety that is the scourge of all people. My love can unblock any congestion and my compassion will ease any depression.

MEDITATION

With your inner vision see the beauty of the geranium and feel yourself drawn towards her form. Become a part of her stem, her leaves and her flowers. The essence of this flower is now a part of you, just as you become a part of this flower. If any of your centres are blocked, your union with this flower, during meditation, will ease congestion or imbalance within the organs of your body. You will be aware of the soothing benefits from the geranium in the days ahead.

JASMINE – In harmony with the Brow, Heart and Sacral Chakras

I am a very ancient flower. I grew within the gardens of Atlantis, Egypt and Persia. My perfume will, therefore, help you to bring back memories of wisdom learnt in past ages. My pungent scent will herald dreams of incarnations past and lives to come. The oil from my flowers will aid all forms of human love, particularly during the act of conception and childbirth. It will also ease grief as my love flows into the heart centre. My perfume will soothe hysteria, insomnia and panic attacks brought on by phobias associated with past incarnations.

MEDITATION

"Visualise yourself in an ancient temple garden. You are bending over a bed of jasmine and picking the blooms. For a moment inhale the scent and let it fill your body. This picture fades and you now find that you are lying on a couch within the temple. The oil from the jasmine flower is being massaged into your skin. Let the remedial properties of the oil pass over any area of your body where you are experiencing distress. Stay here for a short while, and enjoy the peace and beauty that the atmosphere of this healing temple will bring to you. When you return to your everyday life, you will find that any pain or anxiety will have eased.

LAVENDER – aligned with the Brow Chakra

"I have grown in the soil of your planet for many years and my flowers have been used through the Centuries for their mystical properties. My flowers were burnt to ward off evil and to bring back the energies of virtue and goodness. Our bushes are always filled with the essence of the nature spirits, who unite with the elementals working within man's etheric body to strengthen his immune system. It is important that we inhabit your planet, as we can help to combat pollution and lack of pure air. We are able to ease headaches and bring the gift of sleep to anyone suffering from anxiety and restlessness. The pale violet of our flowers will help to balance the flow of energy through all of your chakras and a lavender incense stick will burn off any negativity within these centres.

MEDITATION

Allow your inner sight to gaze upon a lavender bush, and see the nature spirits working within its leaves and flowers. Place your hands over the bush and feel the etheric field that surrounds its form. Unite your own etheric body with the elements of the lavender, so that your energies combine in total harmony. This will balance, uplift and relax you in preparation for your daily tasks.

68

THE LOTUS FLOWER – Blending with the Crown Chakra

"I am a sacred flower beloved of God and the Masters of Wisdom. I float on the still waters of a lake, which is symbolic of the perfected soul of man. I was venerated throughout the Eastern countries of your planet and held in honour by the ancient Mayan race and the Native Americans. I have memories of ancient continents and civilisations long passed away.

"The winds which blow upon my blossoms are as the breath of God and when you meditate upon my image it will bring the love of the Christ spirit into your heart. The sacred centres within your etheric body will start to glow with the light of transformation. The murmur of the sacred AUM will fill your mind with purity and adoration. My petals at the crown of your head will awaken you to the reality of illumination. You will be united with God and become a part of the eternal love that enfolds all of creation. Your physical body will vibrate to the rhythm of the Universe.

"There is a very special angel of light who can be seen standing in the centre of my lotus flower, who is pure unconditional love and divine power. My lotus blossom depicts universal wisdom, unity and understanding which flows directly from the mind of God."

MEDITATION

With your inner mind, stand before a still lake and envisage an open lotus flower. A golden light is pouring from its centre, drawing you into the heart of the blossom. The lotus grows larger and wider, until you are able to step into the centre of this flower. The image changes, and you are now in a golden temple of light. Your teacher from the spiritual realms awaits you, and for a short while you sit and listen to his words of wisdom. You may wish to ask him a question, which he will gladly answer.

On your return to physical life write down all that you have been taught and then given thanks to your teacher for the knowledge which has been given to you.

THE ROSE – In harmony with the Heart Centre.

The nature spirits who work upon my rose bushes bring to man the law of equilibrium. My red rose and my white rose are completely balanced, thereby forming a pink bloom of pure unrestricted love. The thorns on my bushes are symbolic of the strife, which awaits man on his journey to spiritual enlightenment. You may prick and draw blood from your finger, depicting the tears and sorrows on the path of life. The Master Jesus bled from his hands and feet in order that mankind could experience the initiations which would take him back to the heart of God, and his sacrifice brought to man the gift of unconditional love. I am beloved of the Master Jesus, who holds a rose to his heart, as he brings to mankind the realisation that all life vibrates to the law of unconditional love. Once humanity becomes aware of this, most of his problems will fade into significance. I am love, majesty and righteousness. I am purity, so my healing properties will enter into your heart and blood, circulating around the whole of your physical frame.

MEDITATION

Hold a rosebud in your hand. Watch the petals slowly unfold, so that you are looking down into the fully awakened rose. Become aware that you are now seeing the beauty of your own heart centre, your own healing temple of purity and love. All anger, all fear and all resentment melt away, so that a pure and golden light shines out to all

70

the world. This energy is alive and vibrant and 'as you give so shall you receive' is a divine truth. When your meditation is finished you will feel joyful and peacefully content.

THE VIOLET – Blending with the Brow Chakra

"I am sacred to the fairy and angelic kingdom. I am beloved of the ascended Masters, particularly the Master Saint Germaine. I am used by the Archangel Michael when he leads his army of angelic hosts into battle for the spiritual enlightenment of Planet Earth. Although I am quite fragile, I represent the strength of humility and simplicity, which are requirements for the final stages of mans journey to illumination. It is only when man has acquired these attributes that he is able to reach the end of this part of his journey back to God. When you smell my perfume as you enter a room, within your meditations, or in your dream state, know that a Master of wisdom draws close. He will bring you knowledge and awareness of your purpose within this incarnation. You will begin to glimpse how you can be of service to your brothers and sisters, who lift out their arms to you for compassion and understanding.

MEDITATION

Close your eyes and you will find that you have entered a wood in springtime. Look around and see the beauty of the young trees, dressed in the emerging colours of new life. On the grassy banks, between the trunks, are clumps of tiny violets, holding their heads up to catch the first glimmers of an approaching golden sun. Kneel down and cup one of these flowers in your hands, inhaling its fragrance and pausing for silent reflection.

You become aware of a feeling of new birth, the beginning of a new day, the start of a new dawn. There is a hint of raindrops in the air and the smell of a freshly washed earth. As you slowly return from your meditation you feel transformed and ready to accept new challenges. Perhaps you have been considering a change in your life, or you may wish to serve your fellow man in a fresh direction. You know that all things are possible when your heart is open to the inflow of new ideas. Be like the violet and live your life in simple trust and faith.

I hope that my readers have enjoyed these conversations with the nature kingdom that inhabits the trees and flowers. In my travels to other Countries, I always tune in to the Nature Spirits of that land. Their message is always very similar and very positive. They ask that Humanity open up their hearts to unconditional love and to the glory of their own Divinity. They speak of the time to come when all Creation will join together in unity and peace.

Go into the woods and the fields and talk to these etheric beings of light. They will become your friends and your companions. In the very near future man will once more walk, work and play with these devas and denizens of Mother Earth.

Section Three

NATURE SPIRITS OF THE ANIMAL KINGDOM

ANGELS OF LIGHT

Breathing Angels

Breathe with the Angels a voice whispered into my meditation.

They breathe in the tall trees and breathe out the forest's rustling leaves.

Breathe in the crystal brook.

Breathe out the bubbling water.

Breathe out the shape of islands, the golden sands.

Breathe in the seeds, the bulbs of Spring.

Breathe out the perfume of flowers.

Oh – breathe in the dream of the Divine.

Breathe out miracles of healing.

Breathe in the hope of the World.

Breathe out the fire of Truth.

Come – breathe in your perfect form.

Breathe out your angel being.

Breathe out love,

Breathe – just breathe the breath of Angels.

Stephanie Sorrell.

DEVAS OF THE ANIMAL KINGDOM

This is the one part of my book which I couldn't wait to write. I have a great love for the animal kingdom. They are my achilles heel. I cannot bear cruelty to these creatures in any shape or form. I have difficulty listening to tales of torture and misuse on the television, although I know that I must do so, in order to know where to direct healing light and compassion.

My devotion to this realm has enabled me to draw close to the group spirits, or Devas, who guard and watch over every species of beast, bird or fish. Although each creature still has a group soul, many of the domesticated animals are quickly developing the glory of an individual soul. They are moving swiftly up the evolutionary ladder, and may well overtake mankind if humanity does not shake itself free of dogma, fear and hate.

I have had many interesting encounters with the Devas who enfold the animal kingdom. I have discovered that there is no necessity to put down poisons or chemicals if a particular species is becoming a nuisance. For instance if you are being bothered by ants or mice, tune in to the Deva who is guardian of that group, and ask that they be removed from your environment. Explain that you have no wish to harm them, but as they are causing you distress there is a need for their departure. It is always helpful to suggest another area to which they could be discharged. The Deva is always happy to be of service, and delighted that no harm has come to his proteges.

I was in Holland last year, and was asked if I could try and remove some moles who had taken up residence under a newly built patio, in front of a row of houses. When I arrived, the mole traps had already been put in place, and the whole area looked like a scene from a disaster movie.

The slabs on the patio had all lifted up and there were piles of soil all over the place. The moles were having a wonderful time burrowing and excavating their tunnels within the confines of these beautiful gardens. I must admit that when I gazed on this mayhem, I felt very unsure as to whether I could be of assistance. However, after requesting that the mole traps be taken out, I sat down on the patio – surrounded by very curious children – and tuned in to the Mole Deva. With my inner vision I saw a very tall being of light, with the head and features of a mole, together with the paws and long claws. This is the usual picture which I see when meditating on an animal deva – the characteristics of the creature blending in perfectly with the form of the Angel. I explained the problem, and the distress which was being caused by the Moles, and asked that they be removed to a waste piece of land just across the road.

I went home to England and was very pleased to receive a fax telling me that the moles had vacated the gardens. However, a few weeks later I received another message to say "Please try a bit harder, as two moles have come back". I tuned in again to the Deva, and was delighted to learn that the moles had completely vanished and to my knowledge have never returned. I would urge all who read this book to try this experience for themselves. It will not only save the animal kingdom from pain, but will bring a new perception and understanding of the Natures Spirits who inhabit all creation throughout the Universe.

The first thing that I discovered whilst connecting to the animal domain, was that the attributes of these creatures relate quite closely to the characteristics inherent within the sacred centres of man and our planet. By drawing near to the animals and their specific group devas, humanity can evoke their strength and abilities. Many ancient tribes were aware of this fact and, believing that they would take into their bodies the powers of the poor beasts, unfortunately sacrificed them to that end. We have now, hopefully, evolved to a state where we can do this spiritually and not physically. By meditating and sending out the love from our heart centres, we can reflect on the strengths of a particular animal, thereby aiding in our own self-development.

I feel very humble that I have been allowed to glimpse some of the glory of the Animal Devas. Because of my devotion to the animal kingdom, these great Devas have helped me to communicate and share some of the animal's thoughts and feelings. Again I would stress that there is nothing special about these abilities. Everybody can do this. You only need to reach out with love from your heart to make contact with the Devas of this magnificent realm. They will recognise your commitment and help you to comprehend what the animals are trying to tell you.

I was in the Netherlands recently and two good friends came to collect me so that we could walk in the woods together. They arrived very distressed, as they had just seed a dead bird lying in the road. It appeared that the mate was very agitated and was jumping up and down beside the body. They asked me if I could go to the scene and try to ease the sorrow. I readily agreed and we returned to the spot where the dead bird lay. By this time more of its friends were congregated on a nearby rooftop, where they were all chattering and flapping their wings. I tuned into this collection of birds and asked if I could be of assistance.

Within my mind, they thanked me for my concern, but said that they were waiting for the Group Deva to arrive and take the spirit of their dead mate into the light. As I watched, they stayed until this occurred and then flew away. They had paid their respects and given homage to a part of themselves that was joining the great spirit of their species. This may help any Readers who feel great pain, as I do, when they see a dead animal or bird lying by the roadside.

I frequently get distressed calls from owners whose animal friends have gone missing. Cats are particularly prone to this. They will wander for long distances and often get totally lost. I use a special method for drawing them home. I visualise a silver cord, with one end attached to the owner, and the other end fastened to the pet. I close my eyes and tune in to the Deva of that species, asking for his help. I picture the cord tightening and then I slowly visualise the lost animal being drawn back towards the owner. Within hours I have had a telephone call from the owner telling me that the animal has arrived home safe and sound.

One of my greatest joys, as a channel for healing energy, is to work with animals. I run an absent healing group for sick animals, and also have many that come to my Sanctuary for contact healing. They will often commune to me where the pain is, and what has caused the problem. If they are very sick, or very old, they will express their desire to be allowed to pass peacefully into the light. I understand fully how difficult this can be for the owner of the beloved pet. However, there comes a time when we have to consider the animal before our own feelings. After the passing, the beloved pet will joyfully run through fields and gardens on the inner planes, and at night we can go to them in happy friendship. To them our night can be day, and our day can be night. Our treasured pet is not dead, but lives on in the World of Spirit. We can never be separated from those we love, be they animal or human.

People will often ask me if I can see where their companion is in the Spirit Realms, and I can always assure them that their pet is happy and blissfully contented. In my book 'A Healer's Journey into Light' I described a special heaven where all animals are loved and cared for. This is filled with grass, trees, flowers and perfect harmony. Within the light of this realm the lamb truly lies down with the lion.

In this book I also spoke of how receptive animals are to healing. Unlike humans, they are incapable of erecting any barriers or blockage. I always ask for the assistance of our Creator, the Healing Angels and the Group Devas. Anyone who loves animals can do this. Just by placing your hands on the fur of the animal and gently stroking, you can bring healing to that little body. When I visit an animal and ring the bell, it will often greet me on the doorstep and gleefully lead me to the place where I give the healing.

We can all give assistance to the Animal Devas by sending our love across the earth to wherever their Kingdom is suffering. What could be more joyous than to ease the pain of this realm, into which mankind has invoked such agony and disregard. I have grouped several creatures under each of the seven major chakras, as follows:

BASE CHAKRA – Bull, Bear and Dragon.

SACRAL CHAKRA – Fish, Wolf and Bee.

SOLAR PLEXUS CHAKRA – Lion, Cat and Dog.

HEART CHAKRA – Antelope, Swan and Dove.

THROAT CHAKRA – Elephant, Owl and Horse.

BROW CHAKRA – Dolphin and Unicorn.

HEAD CHAKRA – Snake and Eagle.

I will take each of these centres, and animals, in turn. I hope that you will enjoy the experience as much as I have, and that you will take a voyage of discovery yourself into the realms of the animal spirits. I have included two mythical beasts, the dragon and the unicorn, as I believe these creatures did roam our planet in some long forgotten age. When mankind sank deeper into matter they could no longer stand the low vibrations and withdrew from our Earth. Now that humanity is again raising its consciousness, they are drawing close to our world once more.

THE ROOT CENTRE

THE BULL

"I am renowned for my strength and vitality. I am linked with the energy of the oak tree and in olden days I was worshipped for my vigour and sturdiness. I have been with mankind, in some form or another, since you took your first step onto this earth, journeying with you through many ancient civilisations. I have courage to withstand the forces of nature, because I have memory of earthquakes, fire and tempest at a time when your world was cooling in temperature. I am the awakening of power within your base centre. I represent sacrifice as you take your first faltering steps onto the path of light. I am depicted as the benefactor of creation, owing to my virility and potency. I can roar and stamp my hooves on the ground with the first emergence of the sacred fire from the safety of the root chakra, which lies within the centre of the earth at the feet of man. I roam through the rich pastureland, earth and succulent grass of your planet. In this way I am united with the soil. If you, who are human, have difficulty keeping your feet firmly on the ground, then know that I am the symbol of common sense and stability.

"The time is fast approaching, however, when I shall no longer reincarnate upon your globe. Humanity is at last realising that it has no necessity to consume meat. You and your world are advancing in consciousness, and my species will have served their purpose. We will return to our group spirit to await the next turn on the wheel of evolution."

THE BEAR

"I am also representative of power. I walk on four legs, but I am just as happy to stride about on two. This is symbolic of man leaving the crawling stage of babyhood, to grow into the stature of a fully-grown adult. I am symbolic of the changing structure of life and I can help you to adapt to the higher rays of light, which are now pouring down onto Mother Earth. I also represent spiritual abilities, which are lying dormant within your memory. I can help you to awaken these for the glory of your coming transformation. I am very playful and will dance and romp in the spring sunshine, scratching my back on some much-loved tree. I wish all humanity would learn to frolic in the sheer joy of being alive and living on this beautiful planet. Like the Bull, I too will soon disappear form your grasslands. We, as a species, will return to our Group Soul. There we will wait until an opportunity arises for us to take on another form on earth or on some other planet within the Universe. We will, in other words, hibernate in a state of consciousness similar to your dream time. Our lesson, on your globe, was to use power with gentleness and walk with soft feet on the surface of mother earth. This we have achieved, as we would only attack another creature if challenged or in danger."

THE DRAGON

"You see me as a legend, but there was a time, long, long ago, when we inhabited your lands. It was in an age when man walked this earth in the company of angels. We roamed in forests and mountains of primal splendour. Our companions were the natural forces of earth, air, fire and water. I breathe fire from my mouth and roar like the explosion from a volcano. I represent the awakening of the kundalini energy which, when fully aroused from sleep, will take the path up the spine to full enlightenment.

"I also represent luxury and wealth. I am the companion of the alchemist who changes base metals into gold. I am the guardian of treasures and sit at the entrance to many sites throughout your world, where manuscripts of ancient wisdom are buried. One day they will once more see the light of the day. St. George, the patron saint of your blessed Isle of Britain, is seen as conquering the power of the dragon, thereby releasing its fire of spiritual illumination. Your 'sceptred isle' will also know the beauty of the arisen fire, perfectly ignited and controlled."

MEDITATION

You are walking on a carpet of green grass in a meadow filled with buttercups. In front of you is a pure white bull. Do not be afraid, he will do you no harm. Approach him with love and caress his neck and head. His white form denotes purity of motive, and he will lead you to a small cave, outside of which lies a shaggy brown bear. His eyes are soft and welcoming. He nuzzles you with his nose and allows you to stroke his thick fur. He rolls onto his back and kicks his feet in the air. He is showing you how power should be tempered with gentleness and love, and only used for the benefit of humanity. Spend time with these animals and the Devas who enfold them. Listen to what they have to tell you.

As you leave the cave, you see in the distance the outline of a dragon with flaming breath. There is no danger, so you may approach him if you wish. However, if the time is not right, acknowledge his presence and honour his existence. When you are ready, he will always come into your meditations.

THE SACRAL CENTRE

THE FISH

"We swim in water which is the element closely related to the sacral centre of man. We reproduce by spawning in pools and sea beds. The moon, which shines in your night sky, has a great influence upon our mating habits. Owing to the pollution of your rivers and seas, we are quickly beginning to transmute our bodies, in order that our species may survive. Man will also very shortly be going through a process of initiation, whereby he will transmute his own sexual energies. This sacred power will then be used for illumination and the gifts of spirit. Man will learn the law of cycles just as we, the fish, rely on the forces of the tides. This way his procreation will become a natural act of love and not an event of the lower emotions. We lay large numbers of eggs in order to ensure our future existence. Many of our species have a hard struggle to survive, so we are well fitted to inspire man to use strength and determination to overcome the battle of life. We often swim in shoals, very close together. Humanity will also adopt this method in the future, living and sharing his thoughts and possessions with his brother. The waters of life flow through your veins, circulating the spiritual energies, which you will need to burst forth into the golden age of thoughtfulness and harmlessness."

THE WOLF

"Although we are frequently thought of as fearsome and menacing, we are in fact compassionate and co-operative. We live and hunt in packs and have a wonderful instinct for community living.

"The moon and its cycles of behaviour affect our emotions and you will often see us depicted as baying to the moon. In the same way, man lifts up his head and howls in his pain and anger, when his sexual energy is unbalanced and he is automated by his lower nature, instead of listening to his higher mind.

"Legends have always abounded, telling of our ability to change our shape to become half man and half beast. Hence the werewolf. Again, this is indicative of man's battle to overthrow the urges of his lower centres. He struggles and strives; sometimes the beast gets the upper hand, and at other moments his higher consciousness comes into play. We can teach you how to transmute your lower natures to become compassionate and caring, sharing your natural wisdom with your fellow man."

THE BEES

"We are one of the gifts which were given to man at the beginning of creation, by your teachers from Venus. We bring your sustenance with the sweet taste of our honey, which is the result of the hard labour of our workers. When you look into our hives you will see order, loyalty and productiveness. When you study our ways, you will realise that nothing happens by chance; all is held within the wisdom of that great architect whom you know as God. We are symbolic of all activity within the Universe, whose laws are always disciplined and exact. Our Queen Bee signifies your Mother Earth, on whose surface humanity should be working to bring in a future free of hunger and want."

MEDITATION

Imagine that you are swimming in the gentle waters of a calm river. Alongside you are many fish of all shapes and colours. Join them in their dance of life, twisting and shimmering in the sunlit waters. After a short while climb out of the river onto a grassy bank, letting the heat of the summer sun dry your body.

Slowly become aware that you have been joined by a fully grown wolf. Do not be afraid, for she has brought you her cubs to observe. She lays her head in your lap and together you watch the delightful antics of her offspring. They tumble and romp all over the ground, chasing each other round and round in circles. Your heart rejoices in this blissful display of innocence. You realise what a wonderful world lies all about us.

After a time, the wolf and her cubs depart and you are left listening to the sound of bees as they go in and out of the roots of a nearby tree. They bring to you a gift of a honeycomb from their hive. As you eat the sweet nectar be aware of the beauty of creation and the laws of perfect balance. It is only the man who flouts these rules, and soon this too will change. In the coming golden age there will be peace and harmony for all creatures.

THE SOLAR PLEXUS.

I have depicted the Lion, the Cat and the Dog as symbols for this centre. To meet the challenges of the coming age of transformation, man must move swiftly and completely into his heart centre. I find that these three animals portray the qualities of strength, courage, service, loyalty and love, all of which are needed in order to evolve towards the heart. You, my readers, may not agree with me. That's fine, as I would urge you all to reflect and discover your own archetypal animals and their Devas.

The cat and the dog have long been man's companions, and we have much to teach each other. The domestic cat for instance, is a strong healing tool for bringing peace to shattered nerves. A few days ago whilst preparing this chapter, I received a telephone call which badly hurt me. When I replaced the receiver I was shaking with pain and distress. I suddenly felt the touch of a paw, as my beautiful tortoiseshell cat jumped into my lap. Tawny put her small arms around my neck and rubbed her face into my cheek and neck. Within a short while I was again peaceful and tranquil. She had shown me what real love was all about. I was able to send thoughts of love and forgiveness, instead of rancour, to my aggressor.

More and more hospitals are finding that pets, such as cats and dogs, can soothe and comfort the most disturbed of mental patients. Tawny is an old friend from a previous life in Egypt. She immediately recognised my husband and myself when we arrived at our local rescue shelter. We had just lost our cat "Willum", and had heard of a stray cat who needed a home very badly. The rescue centre was full of cats waiting for a kind face, but as soon as we walked through the door a small scraggy bundle jumped from a telephone table onto my shoulder. She proceeded to kiss and nuzzle my chin, purring with delight and recognition. She was the cat we had come to see and she had remembered us from a past incarnation. She knew that she had now come 'home' and was with her rightful owners. Her love, friendship and service from that day has been a joy to experience.

Tawny has her own beautiful Soul Spirit who watches over her, and I am sure that she is well aware of the guidance she receives. Last year she became quite ill and we took her to the Vet. He said that he believed she was suffering from a kidney problem, and to bring her back if she continued to lose weight. We gave her intensive healing and lots of tender loving care. Suddenly my husband noticed that she was disappearing at the same time every evening. We followed her, and watched as she entered my Healing Sanctuary and jumped on the stool in front of the Altar. She stayed there for a quarter of an hour and then left the room. She did this at 10 o' clock each night for about a fortnight. After that period she began to gain weight and recover from her illness. I believe that she was guided to my Healing room by her own special Angel.

A dog will also bring healing to its owner. My husband's stepfather Frank had a Labrador who faithfully sat on his lap and licked his hands and arms. Frank always said that a dog's saliva took away the rheumatics in his hands and wrists. I was a witness to this and can confirm that this was the truth.

Whilst I was in South Africa I made the acquaintance of a beautiful Alsation dog. As soon as I arrived at her home, she licked and welcomed me. For the whole of my stay she very rarely left me. She slept on my bed and went for walks with me. On the morning of my departure there was a great sadness about her. The look in her eyes as I climbed into the car was heart rending. I had a dream the following night, in which I was a male Native American Indian running through the forests. By my side was a huge wolf who was obviously my companion. I recognised the Alsation who I had left behind in South Africa. Our two soul Angels had united us for one short and joyous time during this life. The following is what the group spirits of the animals had to tell me:

THE LION

"I am the herald of strength and courage. I am often pictured as laying down with a lamb, thereby denoting peace. The reason for this is that although I have a tough outer shell and can roar my displeasure, on the inside I can be gentle and placatory. I rule my emotions with fortitude, and can also align myself with the solar sun bringing leadership tempered with maturity. In ancient tribes it was a sign of manhood to hunt and kill me with a spear. In some parts of the world, unfortunately, this act is still performed today. We will never become extinct and leave mankind; we will travel the long road of illumination with you. Once mankind has control over his emotions, so too will the lion. In the distant future we will walk together, man and beast, opening ourselves to the inflow of unconditional love, tempered by dispassionate compassion."

THE CAT

"We have been revered and worshipped in Egypt and reviled and tortured in medieval days. This has also been the path for man, some lives glowing with positivity whilst others have been peppered with negative tribulations. We guard the gates to other planes of existence and can bring to our owner's experiences of past and future incarnations. We will also assist you to withstand the tests and trials necessary to reach the gates of initiation. We are self-controlled of the need to develop dispassionate compassion, tempered with unconditional love, both necessary requisites when the time of initiation draws close. You will often see us staring into space when you can see nothing. We are sometimes witnessing the approach of an advanced teacher, whom we recognise as a brother of the light. We can assist you to activate

91

your light body and to strengthen your energy field, thereby bringing peace and harmony to a frequently ravaged body. We were with you in other ancient civilisations, and many of us are reincarnating with old friends at the approach of the Aquarian age. We have elected to walk with you on the road which will lead us both into a golden future."

THE DOG

"We represent faithfulness, loyalty, companionship and unfailing service. We will help humanity to understand utter devotion. These assets are necessary when making the journey into your heart centres from the solar plexus. We will gladly serve you, acting as guides and helpers for disabled people. This way we will evolve alongside mankind. Do not, however, teach us to be aggressive as this will halt our progression and your own. We will reflect the emotions that you send out to us. If you are sad we will mourn, if you are happy we will know joy. All animals are telepathic and we can read your thoughts, either good or bad. Like our brothers, the cats, we have been with you many times and will reincarnate into a familiar background. Do not weep when we die. Instead be aware that our energy is still with you, and there is a possibility that your next puppy may contain our spirit."

MEDITATION

In your reflections, draw into your meditation a situation where you need courage tempered with love. Now bring into your mind the picture of a lion. Ponder on this image for some while, drawing strength from its presence. The problem that has formed within your inner vision will now seem less severe.

You may feel that you are lacking in energy and are depleted. As before, let the image of a cat form within your meditation. The group spirits who work with this animal will come to your aid and soon you will feel calm and more at peace with yourself. Visualise the light of your own soul enfolding you in its glory.

Before you leave your contemplations, bring into your vision a situation that requires loyalty and friendship. An image of a dog will help you to find a solution. Thank the angels of these animals for their love and help, and return joyfully into the physical world.

THE HEART CENTRE.

THE ANTELOPE

"I portray the first stirrings of the heart when it begins to experience the soft yearnings of love and tenderness. Like the antelope, you may feel very shy and slightly withdrawn as you learn to deal with the inflow of sensitivity to this centre. We are swift of feet and are not dragged down by your perceptions of dogma and prejudices. Mankind can now move about the world quickly and easily, no part of this planet being prohibited. Soon will come the realisation that we are all one, united by the power of the heart and the

93

strength of wisdom flowing from the realms of light. I also, however, embody choice. It is up to you whether you accept what your heart and higher mind have to tell you, or whether you hide behind your own prison of privacy and rejection.

THE SWAN

"I am often seen as serene and unruffled, as I glide across the calm waters of a lake of peace. In your ancient legends I was used to express transformation, and I am indeed indicative of man's renewal as he moves into the heart. True love will overcome all adversity. We, the swans, mate for life, thus portraying faithfulness in any partnership. In spiritual terms, we abandon the desires of our lower selves and move into the glory of our higher consciousness.

"It is said that the sound of a dying swan is matched by the sad tones of a harp in heaven. Our swan-song is a lament for all the suffering of creation on earth. One day this will change to a melody of joy, when all who inhabit the earth have risen into the heart."

THE DOVE

"I am the emblem of love, peace and harmony – all the qualities needed to open up the heart. Unfortunately in past ages, I have been sacrificed in large numbers to placate various idols, especially in the temples of the Hebrews. All who walk the path of light gladly surrender their lower selves in order to reach the heart. Only in this way can humanity learn to love without criticism, accepting his fellow man as part of himself. In the legend of Noah after the flood I was the first bird to see dry land. When Atlantis sank beneath the waves the negativity that had been present in those last days was transformed by the purifying waters into a new beginning. I, the dove, was used as a symbol for a new emergence of innocence, simplicity and purity.

"I am a messenger of divine love, and in the years ahead mankind will recognise why I am used as an emblem by all nations seeking friendship and positive change."

MEDITATION

With your inner eyes, look down upon the earth and see all the fields, meadows and grassland laid out before you. Behold vast herds of antelope running and leaping as they cover the complete surface of our globe. Their hooves are beating a song of love, which is taken up by a flock of white doves who fly up into the sky. They soar into the clouds and around the perimeter of the earth, carrying love into the atmosphere to dispel negative thoughts and pollution. Finally, hold the picture of white swans gliding silently over the waters of every lake and river in the world, carrying peace and harmony in their wake.

THE THROAT CENTRE.

THE ELEPHANT

"As man awakens to the wisdom of spirit, he will realise the meaning of infinity. We, as a species, are timeless. We have evolved from huge mammals, who ruled your planet millions of years ago. We have always existed on your earth, long before your physical bodies have developed a solid skeleton. We have roamed leisurely across your world from pole to pole. It is said that we never forgot, and so we hold within our minds the memory of nature. Everything that has happened to your planet we have seen and digested.

"You respect our size, and yet we can teach you to be gentle and humble. We do not bully and oppress other animals, so why do you strive to subjugate other nations? Use your throats to voice your wish for freedom. Be like us, who lift our trunks to bellow our displeasure at cruelty, poverty and degradation.

"We move around in family groups, with whom we share our food, our loyalty and our love. We unite together for lifetime after lifetime. When you study our attributes, you will hold within your vision a perfect picture of the golden years to come. We will work with you from love, but do not abuse us by making us perform circus tricks. We are your glimpse into the future and should be honoured for our wisdom and spiritual intelligence."

THE OWL

"We express the change which will occur in the minds of men when they move into the energy of their throat centres. We are looked upon as wise, and will assist you to communicate this ancient wisdom for the benefit of your earth.

"We are denizens of the night and will work with the moon to bring to you dreams of the future. Sometimes these visions may be of other planets in other parts of the universe. We understand the cycle of life and death on a level of higher consciousness. We will help you to enter your spiritual bodies, leaving the astral planes far behind you, to travel into the higher spheres of light. We will bring to you knowledge of your inner self. With this awareness will come a clearer indication of your path to illumination. We will take flight and guide you through the forest of your tangled thoughts to a clearer perception of the spiritual universe which is all around you, waiting for the time when the shutters fall away from your eyes."

THE HORSE

"I am spiritual strength and am depicted as a beast of burden. I will assist you to carry your load until you are ready to place it in its true perspective, and harvest the lessons that you have learned. We allow you to ride on our backs to experience the pleasure of freedom. When you are fully awakened to the spiritual world, you will understand the true meaning of liberty. We, together with all of the animal world will begin to converse with you telepathically. This communication will come from the heart and not the brain. This is a lesson, which you must learn before you can move up into the higher centres of the head. Think before you speak, and do not allow any of the words that you utter to hurt or injure another human soul. When we know that you practice harmlessness, then we can draw close to your auras and enjoy the benefit of your companionship. It is said that our horseshoes are lucky.

This is because our feet walk the road of truth and we can help you to move from the dim light of physical existence into the pure light of spirit."

MEDITATION

When you close your eyes envisage a magnificent horse waiting for you to mount onto his back. Do not be afraid, as he will gently lead you into the land of Animal Devas in the realms of light. In this place you will see many different species of beast, living quite happily side by side. Walk amongst them and take particular note of the elephant herds and their families. Enjoy the song of the birds and be aware of a large white barn owl who is sitting on a post in front of you. Stay a short while in the company of these companions. Allow their group spirits to draw close to you, helping you to gain spiritual strength from their qualities.

THE BROW CENTRE

THE DOLPHIN

"I was given to man by the inhabitants of Sirius and Venus. I therefore hold within my mind memories of Worlds filled with the light of love and wisdom. The occupants of these realms have very little form as they are composed of spiritual matter, mainly consisting of the energy of love. This they continually pour down onto your poor afflicted globe. I came to your earth to be your friend, to help you to gain wisdom. Why then do you kill and maim my species for profit and greed? There are some of humanity, fortunately, who recognise the healing power that we bring to you. When you are mentally ill, we can soothe and fill you with happiness and joy. When you laugh, you forget your problems and physical disease becomes less important. We can also assist in the awakening of your intuition, so that you can see beyond your physical limitations. We care about your planet and the environment. When you pollute the seas and the air, we feel the pain of your actions. If you continue with your destruction, we will be withdrawn from the face of your earth. We do, however, hold great hope for your world. The vibrations of physical matter are now much higher than when we first populated the seas of your planet. We feel the energy of love beginning to emerge from all the pandemonium and turmoil of the last hundred years. The time is fast approaching when the workers for the light must overthrow the negativity, which surrounds this globe. Listen to our song, which brings happiness and balance to your weary, careworn world. The spirits of the earth have patience, but they will not wait forever.

THE UNICORN

"I once walked your earth when you were young and innocent, but as your vibrations hardened I could no longer remain. I still come to you in meditations and dreams, in preparation for the time when you will have vanquished your lower passions and I can again return to your physical plane.

"I am symbolic of the grail cup which man has searched for through the ages. What you do not realise is that this is within yourselves. For many incarnations you have been the wounded king, unable to forgive or forget past wrongs. You have been wandering in a wasteland of your own making, and it is only now that you can join the heart with the higher mind and see the vision of your own Divinity. I will help you to understand that all your experiences, both positive and negative, have led you to this point. You are standing at the gates of wisdom, holding within your hearts the light of the Holy Grail. I work very closely with the Archangel Gabriel, who once more will be the Messenger of Hope for humanity as you move forward on the spiral of evolution.

"The horn within the centre of my forehead is the symbol of intuition. As you begin to work with the energies of the fourth dimension, all the gifts of this centre will be open to you. I will come once more into your midst and together we will lead the way into even higher realms of wisdom and discovery."

MEDITATION

Bring to your inner eyes a scene of intense golden light. You may see outlines of hills and trees, but it is as if you are looking through a fine golden mist. Now you observe the contours of a deep blue lake, and swimming towards you is a large grey dolphin, opening his mouth in greeting. Wading beside him is a pure white unicorn, so brilliant that it is difficult to look directly at him. As they reach you, put out your hands in love and friendship. Spend a short time in communion with these two creatures, absorbing the positive vibrations, which they bring to you. Enfold yourself in their cloak of white light, which will help you to raise the vibrations of your everyday life.

THE CROWN CENTRE.

THE SNAKE

"You will see me symbolised in the Caduceus, which is the Greek wand of the healer. When you reach the consciousness of your crown centre, then you will have achieved healing of the self through all the sacred centres of your body. You will have experienced renewal and every cell will sing in unison. When the fire of the snake surges through your chakras I will represent your union with the Christ light, and complete integration with the energies of the universe will have been achieved. The shedding of our skins describes your progression through the various stages of consciousness. You will have reached the Crown by experiencing many cycles of life and death, accepting new lessons and ideas, whilst shaking off old dogmas and outdated beliefs. You will have realised the truth of love is contained in all living creatures down to the smallest blade of grass. We are all one on the evolving spiral of evolution as we reach out to ever higher centres of existence, beyond the comprehension of your limited earthly minds."

THE EAGLE

"My name means 'Spiritual Wisdom'. I soar into the sky, free and triumphant over physical matter. I represent rejuvenation as you step from the material plane into a new life contained in the next dimension. I am the teacher of mysteries and ascension. I am also your link with divine inspiration. The very last of your negative traits to be vanquished will be pride and egotism. I will help you to triumph over this last human entrapment, allowing the full flow of total love and power to crown your head with the thousand petalled lotus."

MEDITATION

Close your eyes and behold a white eagle soaring into a clear blue sky, carrying on his back a coiled snake. No longer does the eagle prey on the snake for food. Instead they unite as one, flying higher and higher into the cloudless sky, passing over mountains, valleys and rivers. They disappear from sight into the golden rays of the sun. they are absorbed into the Christ light which combines the love and power of God. Let this light enfold you, bringing with it the wisdom and enlightenment of the snake and the eagle.

Before leaving this chapter I would like to share with you another experience I have had with the Animal Angels. This involved the Snail and Slug Devas. My husband had a bad heart attack a few years ago, leaving him unable to do any work for several months. His pride and joy is his allotment, upon which reside two large sheds, a green house and an imposing polytunnel. I agreed to do most of the labouring including planting and watering, until he was able to resume gentle weeding and plant care.

We had had a considerable amount of rainfall, so he was understandably disturbed at the thought of slugs and snails marching into his domain and munching on his beloved cabbages. He asked me to buy some slug pellets and scatter over the allotment. Without telling him, I refused, and decided to link in with the Snail Deva and ask for assistance. I have always admired the beauty and intricacy of a snail, particularly the symmetry of the home that it carries on its back. The Deva of this species was no exception; the whole body of this exquisite angel was encased in a spiral shell, radiating light, and on its head were two perfect antennae. I explained the situation, and asked that the snails and slugs be kept off the lands as, on his return to health, my husband would surely deliver a death notice in the form of slug killer.

Despite the very showery nights, I was delighted to discover that the trails of slime from the snails were leading onto vacant overgrown plots and not onto our allotment. When Peter returned to his empire, he congratulated me on the good job I had done, as none of his plants were marked by the devastation from hungry mouths. I told him of my deception, and he had great difficulty in believing my story, although the proof was staring him in the face. Nonetheless, it is the truth and I know that this method will work with all creatures, be they mice, ants or wasps. Nature spirits and devas are only too willing to help us to transform our gardens and homes into areas of Paradise. We only have to tune in to their energy and ask for their assistance.

My journey into the realms of the Animals Spirits is complete. I hope that you have enjoyed my links with the many Group Spirits, which abound within that kingdom. I invite you also to have fun and pleasure whilst exploring this realm for yourselves. Experience the joy and happiness that my meditations have brought to me. To know total unity with all domains is to find a small fragment of God's perfection, and to grasp a tiny part of his plan for the dwellers on this Planet.

Section Four

NATURE SPIRITS OF THE MINERAL KINGDOM

I have already spoken of the angelic presence within trees and animals, and the rocks of the Earth are no exception. They too have their own special Devas and Nature Spirits who live in stones, crystals and the Earth itself. Let the rocks and the Earth talk to you, and you will become a part of the heart and mind of GAIA, our Planetary Mother, in whom we live and breathe and have our being. You might have an ancient site somewhere near to where you live, with standing stones or ancient track. If you stand within this area, close your eyes and touch one of these fragments of our earth; they will respond by bringing you visions of ancient wisdom and bygone ages. They will also awaken your memory as to who you are, why you are here and what lies ahead for humanity.

England, at this present time, seems to be the target for a considerable number of what are called "crop circles". Amazing and complicated geometrical shapes appear in the corn fields during the summer months, particularly in the southern half of Britain.

These crop circles are enormous in length and breadth, sometimes taking up the whole side of a hill, and are geometrically accurate to the nearest inch. No human hand could have made these. A few small circles may be fakes, but generally it would take 200 people, leaning out of helicopters to form them. So who made them? What has formed their perfect symmetry? I believe, and some experts agree with me, that a considerable number are created and shaped by Mother Earth herself.

Last year, I was privileged to enter a circle of great beauty and complexity. If you look on the internet under crop circles/crop circle connector/Alton Barnes July 11, 1997 you can see how magnificent and awe-inspiring it is. My friend Joan Fugeman and myself lay in the centre area with our faces in the earth and just soaked up all the love and compassion which was flowing into us. I felt that the shape of this crop circle signified the Christ Grid, or ring of divine love that has been created around our Earth. Farmers say that these circles are formed very quickly. One particular Farmer tells the tale of how he was working on his land at midnight and went back to the farmhouse for a quick cup of coffee. On returning to his fields 20 minutes later a corn circle had been produced.

There are videos that show small lights bouncing about the meadows. These small lights are exactly the same phenomena that I saw as a child when I pictured Nature Spirits. So are these tiny beings of light performing the work of Mother Earth? I believe so.

I believe that she is talking to us in her own language, the language of the Universe. These wonderful geometric shapes are assisting humanity to raise its consciousness. Most people who enter a circle will talk of various experiences. When meditating they may be aware of joy or hear a slight buzzing noise. Others, who enter out of curiosity, often feel dizzy or nauseous. It is an encounter I would urge all to share, who wish to unite with the wisdom of the Earth Mother.

I hope that the last part of this book will encourage you to experience the energies of various crystals. Experiment and discover their beauty for yourselves. Whenever I am taking a Workshop I give a small piece of either rose or amethyst quartz crystal to each participant. I ask them to hold these to their hearts, uniting with the little angelic entity within the crystal and then program it with unconditional love and peace. I then ask them to go out in the weeks ahead and place this tiny crystal anywhere that may feel negative. In this way, the crystal will transform negative to positive and another small part of the Earth will have been cleansed.

For several years I traveled through England selling craft work. I visited many shopping centres where the energy was less than perfect. I always performed this ritual and felt the raising in vibration over the next few days.

Also at my Workshops I will make a circle of either small clear quartz or rose quartz crystals. These crystals have always been previously placed on the altar within my Sanctuary, so that love and healing is energised within them. I then invite any participants to sit in the centre of this circle and experience the love and healing radiating from the stones.

I would invite all my Readers to make their own circles, tuning into the joy and love which has been formed in the heart of GAIA, our glorious Earth Mother, who has created such beauty within her physical body.

As we move into the Aquarian age, more and more secrets are being revealed to us by Mother Earth herself. Interest in the qualities of crystal and gemstones are spreading throughout the world, and the many properties of these beautiful formations are becoming recognised and utilized by sensitives. This knowledge is not new to mankind as we have all used the power of these stones in long forgotten ancient civilisations. In Atlantis, for instance, several huge crystals were used to generate power to the inhabitants of towns and villages. When humanity is ready, knowledge of these resources of energy will reappear once more upon the surface of our planet.

The Greek interpretation for crystals is ice and they were known as 'frozen water from the heavens'. Our reaction to these stones varies according to our birth sign and the cosmic rays, which are pouring into our bodies. Each piece of crystal contains a tiny entity who is the representative for a wondrous group spirit who overshadows that particular variety of stone.

I have always found that crystals that have been given to me as gifts have a special significance. They have been chosen with thought and when I hold them in my hands they immediately invoke a feeling of warmth and love. This was very much the case when I received a beautiful piece of quartz crystal from a friend of mine in Australia. She explained that it had come from India, where it had been cut from the earth with reverence and love. This became very clear when I held it in my hands as the energy of unconditional love was just pouring from it. Everybody who has touched it has felt the same vibration. What a pity that more crystal miners and importers do not have the same integrity. I am becoming very alarmed that mankind is now ransacking the earth for more and more huge caverns of crystals for greed and power. We do not, at this present time, have to own enormous slabs of crystals in order to behold their power. We can get just the same result from a tiny piece of stone, as from a gigantic rock.

Within the following pages, I have again written about my contemplations with the Nature Spirits who enfold the mineral kingdom. Once more I have included a short meditation which you may find helpful.

AMETHYST – Aligned with the Heart and Crown Centres

"I am a Deva of the seventh ray. I have been waiting in the earth for the dawn of the approaching age. You admire me for my beauty and colour that denotes strength and determination. Within your chakras I am able to transfer love from the heart to the head, balancing all your emotions with power from the crown centre. I can bring you peace and the comfort of deep sleep. From this sleep will come clear realisation of your true potential as a spiritual being encased in the solidity of matter. Hold me in your hands and I will help you to form a clear link with the highest spiritual realms. My angels form an arc of clear perception and love, which will enhance any ritual used for healing. This love will enfold your patients, helping to clear and remove impurities and blockages. I am the river of life within the mineral kingdom. You have helped to fashion my structure whilst resting between lives, so we are linked with the past, the present and the future. My message for mankind is 'Peace and health to all men. Cease all strife and struggle and embrace the strength of your own individual soul'."

MEDITATION

Hold this stone between your hands and visualise a clear amethyst lake. See a white swan sailing serenely across the surface. This is your soul absorbing the properties of the amethyst crystal. Feel a deep and abiding peace enter your heart and flow through your bloodstream, bringing tranquility and clear vision to every part of your body. All the separate atoms of your frame are in harmony. Each one is filled with a perfect understanding of spiritual love. From this moment, all dross and blockages will slowly dissolve from your etheric and physical bodies.

AMBER – Affiliated with the Solar Plexus and Throat Centres.

"I am the Deva of the amber stone, which is composed of fosilized wood. I, therefore, have a memory of times long gone when I grew in the heat of Lemuria and in the cool glades of Atlantis. I grew on the banks of the Nile in Egypt and protected the druids in ancient Britain. When you hold me in your hands I will reveal past lives to you. I will help you to come to terms with emotions brought through from older days and I can assist you to alleviate health problems of a karmic nature. Genetic afflictions, asthma, respiratory ailments and venereal diseases can all be eased with the help of the amber vibrations. My angels are now free from the restrictions of the Piscean age, and can work with the Lords of Karma to slowly bring to a halt the wheel of rebirth for many souls. The way is open for evolved mankind to read the akashic records. The recording angels hold the amber stone within their hearts bringing the message to humanity of self-forgiveness.

Only then can you learn from past mistakes and move upwards on your evolutionary journey. Your quest will eventually take you out into the universe, onto other stars and planets. There is nothing that mankind cannot achieve. He is becoming limitless".

MEDITATION

Hold the amber in your hands and enter a temple of pure amber light. The golden colour is symbolic of spiritual advancement. In front of you is a screen on which you see flashes of past centuries, some scenes may even be familiar to you. The whole panorama of mans' history can be revealed in this way. You may even see the universe laid out before you and take a step out into the glory of the stars. The amber light will lead and protect you.

CLEAR QUARTZ – In harmony with the Brow and Crown Chakras

(Whilst studying the structure of clear quartz crystal, I came across several tales which told of the power of this stone to dematerialize and ultimately to materialize again.

113

I did not believe these stories until I experienced an amazing occurrence within my own life. I was travelling to America and took with me a clear quartz crystal wand, which I usually carry when I set forth on a journey. I popped it into an inside pocket in my suitcase, where I felt that it would be safe.

When I reached my destination I needed to use this crystal, so I reached into my case to take it out of its resting-place. My fingers found only an empty space – no crystal wand. To my consternation the stone was nowhere to be seen. I searched my luggage inch by inch, to no avail. I assumed that the impossible had happened and that my crystal had dropped out somewhere and was lost. Unfortunately, on my return to England my suitcase did not follow me – it went walkabout in America for two weeks.

When I was at last reunited with my clothes, I instantly noticed a bulge in the pocket where I knew that I had previously placed my crystal. To my astonishment, there it was safe and sound despite the fact that I had searched that hiding place three times before. I can only think that it had no desire to travel with me on that particular trip. It had vanished from my sight until my suitcase had returned to familiar surroundings – strange but true.

The following is the message that I received from the entity, which works with the vibrations within the clear quartz crystal:

"Although I have grown for millions of years within the safe warmth of the earth, I am also very much at home on the surface of this planet basking in the light of the sun. I am, for that reason, able to tap deep into your inner consciousness as well as understand the thoughts, which come from your outer material mind. I can help you to bring to the surface ideas and intuitive teachings from your higher self. I am a wonderful emissary for meditation, enabling the head centres to open and receive the wisdom of the higher spiritual planes.

"I am able to fathom the darkness of Hades, so I am a powerful instrument for assisting in the safe transition of a soul at death into the realms of light. I also work with the Lords of Karma and can, in meditation, bring a clear perception of previous errors or virtues.

MEDITATION

As you hold the clear quartz crystal within your hands, you will find yourself in the Halls of Wisdom which lie on the higher mental planes. Wander through the vast libraries, until you feel drawn to a particular book. Sit for a while and ponder on the contents of this volume, turning the pages slowly one by one. When you return from your meditation, write down in a notebook all the things that you can remember reading from that ancient manuscript. You will find that your mind is much more positive, and that any negative thoughts have been transmuted into living energies of light.

CITRINE – Synonymous with the Solar Plexus and Heart Centres.

"I am a member of the quartz family, with the additional strength of iron traces in my composition. Iron is necessary for your bloodstream, making me an ideal instrument for the healing of any blood disorders. I am, therefore, able to alleviate skin eruptions as well as anemia.

"I am also known as the crystal for happiness. I can promote laughter, and bring to anybody holding me a more a positive outlook. I am an ideal stone to carry on your person to encourage goodwill to all men. If you are having a personal problem, hold me in your hand and ask the soul of your aggressor to help to make peace with you. In this way harmony will prevail. I can also be used to bring peace to countries of the world in the same way. Just ask that the souls of the warring continents may meet in harmony.

"It is said that I am ruled by the Sun, and I can assist you to develop courage and mastery over any situation. I will also come to the aid of anyone with suicidal tendencies.

"I am also known as the stone of abundance. I will assist in the acquisition of money when a situation becomes critical, but this does not mean that I will abet the accumulation of wealth. I can, however, bring towards you the wisdom to deal practically with the energy of money.

MEDITATION

When you hold this crystal, you will find that you are in an atmosphere of fun and laughter. It may be a wedding, an engagement party or a festival of celebration. There is lots of music and dancing. You may even see nature spirits joining in the merriment. Enter into the gaiety and allow the joyousness to flow through your veins. Feel alive and smiling and let your voice sing a song of praise to all creation.

DIAMOND – Associated with the Crown Chakra.

"I am the gem of purity, faithfulness and spiritual power. Unfortunately man has sought me for avaricious ends, leading to greed and an overpowering obsession with wealth. Mother Earth has been plundered and scarred in the mad rush to dig me out of the ground. This is not of my choosing and eventually man will have to pay back to the earth what he has taken.

"I can lead you to the heights of enlightenment and to union with your higher self. Because of my spiritual power I can aid in the combating of evil. I can dispel fear and end quarrels.

"When worn with a wedding ring I am able to bring joyous union and magical sexual love to that marriage. My energy will add endurance to any situation and when I am worn on the body, I can strengthen bones within the human skeleton. I am also a Master Healer for all situations.

MEDITATION

As you sit quietly you will see a diamond forming within your inner vision. It is revolving and throwing off all the colours of the spectrum. Pick one particular facet and colour, letting it flow into your mind and heart. You will slowly become aware of a particular part of your life which needs attention. Reflect on this and begin to see the negative aspects changing to positive. Bring this through into your own personal life at the end of the meditation.

EMERALD – In harmony with the Heart Centre

"I am the teacher of unconditional love. I am the gemstone that will bring balance to your soul. I am useful for any disease of the body caused by disharmony. I represent the scales of justice, so am the Messenger of Wisdom. Solomon placed me in his Temples of Judgement and in his Chambers where decisions of state were made.

"I am also the Keeper of Secrets. Gaze into my depths and discover the mysteries of the Universe. I am also the slayer of delusion and if held whilst meditating I will induce a clear and precise picture of the higher astral planes.

"I will help at childbirth and will keep the wearer of my stone forever young. It is said that I hold the secret of eternal youth, but this is an inner rejuvenation rather than a physical one.

MEDITATION

Look into the surface of an emerald and ask to be taken anywhere within the upper mental planes. Visit the kingdom of children or of animals. Walk in the fields of knowledge and talk to teachers and wise men. Visit friends and relatives who have passed into the light. Stroke and fondle well-remembered animals from earlier years. You will bring back from your meditation a lucid and perfect recollection of where you have been and what you have seen.

GARNET – Aligned with the Base and Sacral Centres.

"I am the bringer of good fortune. I will turn daydreams into reality. Put me under your pillow at night and I will enable you to interpret your dreams. The deep colour red of fire is built into my makeup, and is indicative of my association of the kundalini fire both in mankind and the planet earth. I will help with the safe alignment of this energy, but only when the recipient is ready for the passage of the serpent fire through the chakra system.

"I am also able to assist humanity with sexual problems, helping to bring balance to this area of high emotions. I will generate healing to the reproductive organs as well as to the diseases that afflict this area. I will teach mankind that they are spiritual beings inhabiting physical bodies. I can also be used to dispel pollution within the bowels of mother earth."

MEDITATION

Visualise a large garnet held over this globe which we call earth. See the energy from the garnet spreading through rivers, seas, forests, mountains, fields and meadows. Behold it clearing pollution and decay. Envisage the Earth as it was at the dawn of history, pure and unspoiled by the hand of man. Look at the beauty of the trees and grassland, at a time when our planet was virginal and unimpaired by the excesses and greed of the human race.

JADE – In Harmony with the Heart Chakra.

"I can be your protector and guide, both in this world and the next. Although I am the bringer of a long life, if held at death I can promote a peaceful passing and will take the spirit straight into the tunnel of light. I will also slow down the process of decay, so I am invaluable in preserving bodies awaiting cremation or burial. I was used for this purpose in ancient Egypt.

"I will also aid in balancing the energies flowing through the chakra system. Hence the wide use of jade in eastern countries where the development of the chakra is a well- known practice.

MEDITATION

Hold a piece of this beautiful green jade within your hands and visualise energy flowing through your chakras. See each centre perfectly balanced, until there is complete harmony from the crown of your head to the base of your spine. Come back from your meditation feeling refreshed and invigorated. Any part of your body where there is ill health should also be revitalised and fortified. All is peace. All is harmony."

LAPIS LAZULI – Aligned to the Throat and Brow Chakras.

"I reflect the blue of the night sky and am aligned with the moon. For this reason I can facilitate sleep, bringing a refreshing and healing nights repose. I am associated with the brow chakra and the third eye, so I am able to aid in the development of psychic abilities. I can help in the healing of metal problems and will take away fear.

"I can assist with any disease affiliated with the thyroid gland and am strongly aligned with the throat centre. I am therefore a powerful influence on all creative activity.

"I was used for the tablets of stone which Moses brought down from the mountain top. I was also worn over the brow centre in the days of Atlantis and ancient Egypt. I adorned the arms of the Oracles of Greece, as an amulet for enhancing the psychic energies flowing through their bodies."

MEDITATION

Imagine that you are gazing onto the surface of a piece of lapis lazuli. It is as if you are looking into a whirlwind of emotions. All around you a tempest is raging, with sheet lightening illuminating a darkened sky. In the centre of the whirlwind is the eye of the storm, a place of peace and serenity. You are now standing on this exact spot. The turmoil and bedlam that is swirling about you has no power to touch you. Nothing can trouble the calmness of your soul, no unrest can ruffle the tranquillity of your mind. When your meditation is completes you realise that this composure will be a part of you for the rest of your life. There is always an 'eye of the storm' in every situation.

MOONSTONE – Affiliated with the Sacral Chakra

"I have been given this name because my appearance is milky like the moon. The light and energy from this celestial body flows through my vehicle. I reflect the feminine aspect of the moon, together with the mystery associated with darkness and light. I can, therefore, be carried as a talisman of good fortune.

"I can help to ease the pains associated with female procreation as well as aiding at the time of childbirth. I delight in the beauty of human love and I will assist in the balancing of emotions that tear at the heart of unrequited love. I am a jewel to be exchanged by lovers and romantics who walk the stony path of physical love and sexual fulfilment. In advanced souls I will aid the transmutation of these sexual energies into the higher centres."

MEDITATION

Relax and hold a small piece of moonstone to your heart centre. It is night time and the rays of the moon are pouring down upon you. Let these energies be absorbed into your body, balancing all negativity within your sacral centre. Let the rays of moonlight awaken the intuitive part of your nature, bringing awareness of your higher self and answers from the higher mental plane. You are bathed in the light of Christ.

OBSIDION – Associated with the Base Chakra.

"I am known as a protection stone which guards against battles within yourself, and wars between countries. The minerals, which lie deep in the earth have been turned into instruments of destruction by mankind. I can balance this evil by drawing to the world the Angels of Peace. My energy is male, so I can project strong vibrations, which must only be used for good. I can help to balance the kundalini chakra and the solar plexus at this period in mans' history when he is moving from the Piscean into the Aquarian Age. These shifts in consciousness are causing your immune systems to over-react and I will help you to make this transition without strife and torment. I can also assist in the transformation of your DNA structure, which is altering to allow your body to absorb the energies of this new age."

MEDITATION

Hold this stone against your heart and bring into your inner vision any country or person who is battling against negative forces. Centre your thoughts on tranquility and love. See harmony return to all situations enabling peace to reign supreme. As the energies of light flow into your body, allow them to transform you into a vessel of pure serenity.

OPAL – Synonymous with the Brow and Crown Centres

"Not everyone can wear the splendour of my stone as I am the Bringer of Truth, which is not easy for some of humanity to come to terms with, particularly when related to themselves. I invoke honesty and freedom from corruption, so do not expect to keep me round your neck if you are hypocritical and deceitful. If you use me well however, I will help you to understand your inner feelings. I will awaken your head centres, together with the stimulation of your pineal and pituitary glands. I will help you to 'see' with your third eye and bring relief to your physical eyes. The innocence of children can also be glimpsed within my depths.

MEDITATION

Only use this stone if you wish to see a mirror of yourself, reflecting the darkness and the light. Hold it to your eyes and gaze into its depths and be aware of a clear perception of your higher and lower self. You will find that this meditation will help to bring you balance and a feeling of humbleness as you realise that you are indeed a much-loved child of God. Before returning to reality, see a circle of Christ light enfolding you. Bring back with you the knowledge that we all travel the same path to initiation, each one of us experiencing similar tests and trials. An opal is a stone that represents the ascended Masters who watch over the evolution of mankind. They see every faltering footstep that we take as we walk on the inner path of light.

ROSE QUARTZ - In harmony with the Heart Chakra.

"I am the stone of pure unconditional love. My energy flows into your heart, bringing joy and light to all the other chakras of your body. I carry compassion to comfort hurt bodies and minds, allowing the waters of forgiveness to enter as a balm for many tormented souls. When the tongue has let forth its barbs, I am the solvent that succours and soothes. Where imperfections abound, I will wash them away in the pink light of my radiance. Nothing can stand against the power of love, not death, not fear, not anger and not evil. I am the stone for the Archangels and Messengers of Love, who direct and govern your Universe."

MEDITATION

Imagine that a rose quartz crystal is embedded in the cave of your heart. Let the vibrations flow out into the world, healing, comforting and transmitting pure unconditional love. Allow these rays to envelope countries, people and all God's creatures. Hold within your vision a picture of the world free from strife, an earth that is once more a paradise for angels and men. See yourself sitting within a circle of rose quartz crystals and feel the unconditional love which the Devas of these stones pour out to you."

RUBY – Aligned with the Base and Heart Centres.

"I come from the sun and the redness of my jewel brings healing to the blood stream. I can neutralise poison and am a very powerful stone for use on the immune system.

"I give forth strong male energies, which can combat evil and negativity, particularly those vices which have been brought through from Lemuria and Atlantis. I am used by the Archangel Michael and his army of angels, who work to overcome darkness and bring light to your much abused planet."

MEDITATION

Hold a ruby in your outstretched hands towards the sun, allowing the red rays of this jewel to permeate the atmosphere of the earth. Visualise the darkness that surrounds your planet giving way to the brilliance of the Christ light. See the thought-forms that poison your globe slowly dissolve, as the ruby rays sink deeper into the earth. Look at the world as it will be in the future, an orb of pure light, a perfected vehicle for the mighty spiritual being who uses it as his physical expression.

129

SAPPHIRE – Affiliated with the Heart and Brow Centres

"I am delighted to be worn as an engagement ring by lovers, as I am the symbol for utter devotion and faithfulness. When I look at humanity I feel immense sympathy and I am an ideal stone for any warm-hearted person who wishes to enfold all suffering creatures within their arms. I am love, I am empathy, I AM. I hear no evil, I see no evil, I speak no evil. I am the gem of the philanthropist, and the dispenser of charity who succours the wandering lambs of God's creation. I will bring back to the fold the roving black sheep, the vagrant and the vagabond.

"I can invoke chastity and purity, and I can be placed on the body to bring down temperatures, inflammations and skin eruptions."

MEDITATION

Hold a sapphire stone to your heart and let it shine out into the world, bringing succour ands hope to the homeless, the refugees, the forlorn and the helpless. Let the light from this gem guide all who have lost their way into a safe haven. Reflect on the Aquarian age being a period when no man or animal lacks food, shelter or warmth. Let the sapphire be a symbol of mans' humanity to man.

130

SELENITE – Powerfully connected with the Crown Chakra. (I was once given a small piece of selenite by a friend in America. He told me that it would bring change into my life. From that moment I never looked back; my whole life was turned upside down and I found myself tackling situations which I would never have imagined could happen. I began to write books and articles, give interviews and teach at workshops and lectures around the world). This is what the spirit of the selenite stone says to me:

"I am the crystal for change on all levels and areas of consciousness, both for mankind and for the planet earth. It is of great importance that when you unite with my energy you must be ready and willing for these shifts to occur. I am a stone that will take you up into the higher centres above your crown, and help humanity to make the transition into the 'Golden Age' I will assist in the bending of the bough so that it does not snap and break under the pressure of change. I will work with the Christ light as it grows stronger on your earth plane. I AM LIGHT, I AM LIGHT, I AM LIGHT."

MEDITATION

Only meditate with the selenite crystal if you welcome change. Remember the words used by all disciples 'Not my will dear God, but Thine'. Come to a point in your contemplations where all is silent. Hold a small piece of selenite and let the energies flow through all your chakras. Raise your consciousness to the highest point of light and be filled with love, power and wisdom from the realms of spirit. Ask that God's protection may enfold you in the weeks ahead. I wish all who are inspired by the selenite, a joyous and happy future, working for the benefit of creation as we move from the Piscean Age into the golden rays of the next glorious era.

TIGER'S EYE – Associated with the Solar Plexus and Throat Centres

'Tiger, tiger, shining bright in the forests of the night'.

"I am sleek and stealthy and can bring to you self love, confidence in your abilities and strength to overcome all of life's problems. I am related to your solar plexus and throat chakras and because I bring to you self worth, I am an ideal healer for asthma and the digestive system. I will help you to breathe correctly, taking into your lungs the love and wisdom of God and expelling these virtues into your surrounding area. I will also draw towards the wearer of tiger's eye the gifts of spirit, which have been earned through service during many previous incarnations."

MEDITATION

Try to find a tiger's eye that has been set into a ring and wear it on your finger during meditation. Breathe in deeply, allowing the light of love to enter your lungs, and then breathe out this brilliance so that it encircles your whole body. Recognise that you are a child of God, a perfect creation, made into the image of His love. Be proud therefore of who you are, and what you have achieved. Have confidence in yourself and the future. Know that all is well – there is nothing to fear – and that all is held within the heart and mind of God.

TOPAZ – Related to the Throat Centre.

"I am a jewel which will link you to the higher astral planes. Place me under your pillow at night, and I will assist in bringing to you clear, untroubled dreams. I will take you to many of the beautiful places that abound within the higher astral levels. You will see and hear wonderful music, you will wander in the lands of children and animals and you will participate in the healing temples within the gardens of rest.

"I will also protect all travelers who wander on the physical surface of your planet earth. Hold me in your pocket and I will guard you against misfortune and sudden accident when you leave your home to walk down the avenues of life.

MEDITATION

Hold this stone against your heart centre and let your inner vision explore the wonders of the spiritual world. Just relax and let the visions of beauty and contentment pass in front of your gaze. If you have a fear of travelling, let the rays from the topaz surround you and the vehicle in which you are expecting to journey. You will come back from your meditation at peace with yourself and no dread of what tomorrow may hold. At the finish of your reflections, encircle your body in a cloak of pure white light.

TOURMALINE – In Harmony with the Brow Chakra.

"I am known as the cleanser of the mineral kingdom. My energies will flow through you, purifying every centre and atom of your physical and etheric bodies. I am, therefore, a powerful healer for all obstructions and diseases on every level of consciousness. I can also alleviate mental blockages and I am ideal for all forms of psychiatric disorders emanating from the mental planes. I will soothe, comfort and cleanse minds that have become hardened and 'one-pointed', washing away all negative and obtrusive thoughtforms."

MEDITATION

Use this stone to visualise any blockages that have occurred within your mind. Where you know that you have been stubborn and hard-headed, let the situation be held in the energy of the tourmaline crystal. Know that every situation can be worked out for the benefit of both parties. This is particularly useful if you have had a difference of opinion with neighbours or squabbling relatives.

These are a but a few of the crystals who wait on the threshold of discovery for man to realise their importance in the evolution of humankind. Hold them with love my friends and you will unlock their many secrets. They will unveil their mystery and their magnificence, allowing you to glimpse the reflective brilliance of their own path to illumination.

Before leaving this book, I must share with you a very profound experience that I had in South Africa. A very special friend, Su Macintyre, and myself went to the top of Table Mountain early one morning. It was very clear, as the mountain was not clothed in its usual tablecloth of mist. The first thing I saw was an elf sitting on a rock, and then Su noticed a pink haze beginning to form around the perimeter of the mountain. Suddenly, to our utter amazement, the Guardian of the Mountain showed himself to us. We saw vast streams of red and orange colours pouring up into sky. We were beholding the strength and vigour of this mighty angelic entity.

Every Mountain, Valley, Forest and Sea has these potent Guardians who oversee their growth and development. They guard their secrets and watch over the nature spirits who work on their etheric bodies. When we again learn to connect with these tremendous forces, we can work together for the glory of Mother Earth.

Before we complete this journey into the realms of angel enchantment, there are two more vessels of light to whom I must pay homage. One is the great God Pan, who enfolds all etheric life within his aura and whose physical body takes the form of a magnificent centaur, half man, half horse. The other is the Spirit of the Earth, whose picture hangs in my lounge, where I can gaze upon her beauty as I go about my daily tasks. This painting shows the Spirit of the Earth as a young girl with flowing hair. She is holding the world in her arms and enfolded within her gown are many animals and creatures of the Earth. Water is pouring from her arms along with the fishes of the deep. Her hair is full of birds and her feet are guarding rabbits and foxes. This is how I have always visualised her within my meditations and healing prayers.

These two exalted beings give to the readers of my book this final message:

"It is a long time since mankind has recognised and been aware of our presence. We have been saddened by your disregard, and complete ignorance of our natural laws. Many animals and nature spirits have left your lands, and parts of your glorious globe have become uninhabitable.

"Now, however, you are awakening and opening your eyes to the vision of your once illustrious planet. Again you are observing the spirits of nature and the magnificence of the animal and tree devas. This gladdens our hearts, that once more we can clasp hands and walk together in peace and harmony. We ask that all who see us through eyes of splendour, instruct their younger brothers in the necessity to replenish that which has been lost. In this way we can come together in consciousness, allowing this world to shift in vibration without the need for vast earth changes and chaos.

"We leave you now, asking that you bring us into your thoughts and meditations, allowing our hearts to mingle in unconditional love for all creation."

I do hope that you have enjoyed this book on Angels, and that it will help you to discover the joy and love which these beings of light can bring into your life.

If you feel that you would like to host one of my Workshops, or would just like to write to me, please send a stamped, addressed envelope to:

Lorna Todd,
P.O. Box 1109,
Portslade,
Brighton,
BN42 4PP
England